POACHERS' TALES

POACHERS' TALES

JOHN HUMPHREYS

Illustrations by John Paley

David & Charles

BY THE SAME AUTHOR

Living Off the Land
Hides, Calls and Decoys
The Sportsman Head to Toe
Modern Pigeon Shooting
Stanley Duncan, Wildfowler
The Shooting Handbook (Ed)
The Do-It-Yourself-Gameshoot
Learning to Shoot
The Woods Belong to Me (Ed)
Hunter's Fen
Shooting Pigeons
The Country Sportsman's Record Book & Journal
The Complete Gundog

An apparently innocent walking-stick was not always what it seemed

British Library Cataloguing in Publication Data
Humphreys, John
  Poachers' tales.
  1. Title
  639,092

  ISBN 0-7153-9918-7

Text: © John Humphreys 1991
Illustrations: © John Paley 1991
First published 1991
Reprinted 1992

Printed in Italy by New Interlitho SpA, Milan
for David & Charles
Brunel House   Newton Abbot   Devon

CONTENTS

'A Poacher is but a Gamekeeper turned inside out'

INTRODUCTION

With greedy eye he looked on all he saw.
He know not justice and he laughed at law:
On all he marked, he stretched his ready hand,
He fished by water and he filched by land.

CRABBE

The poe-faced and the dismissive felt it a bad idea. A book on poaching? A scurrilous work which might in some way glorify that awful profession and cause offence to those keepers who had suffered at their hands, a book to exasperate every legitimate shooter in the land and cause outrage to those who have lost loved ones to the hands of game stealers? The more enlightened were not so concerned, and ironically it was the keepers themselves who furnished me with a great deal of material of first-hand encounters, tales of fierce affrays in the moonlit corridors in the woodland and yarns of old characters still above the sod who knew a thing or two more than was proper for a good churchgoer.

The small handful of objections came from the new breed of urban rustic, those who run clay shoots for hospitality days and whose real knowledge of the warp, weft and slow rhythms of the countryside could be written on a pin-head with a felt-tipped pen. Those closer to the soil know that there is more than one species of poacher; their ranks include the noblest in the land – no names, no pack drill, for only a cad would kiss and tell – to shiftless thugs and thieves to whom a stolen bird is no more than barterable loot to be traded as quickly and cynically as the proceeds of their burglary the night before.

In between lies a great army of mostly harmless folk no better and no worse than the man next door, but who have retained the ancient hunting instinct and atavistic lawlessness which would not be snuffed out in an EEC beaurocratised, Britain. They could not accept the man-made rule which bestowed ownership to the birds of the air and the beasts of the field which ran and flew hither and thither as they wished, crossing numerous boundaries in a day and changing masters as many times. They had reckoned that the 'haves' made laws to protect what they think they own from the depredations of the 'have-nots' – but has it not always been thus?

Many of the tales which follow relate to the days of Victorian England; those times which seem rustic and comfortable idylls when viewed from the safe distance of a century later. In fact the village folk were very much at the whim of a potentially tyrannical squirearchy which passed its own draconian Game Laws to protect its personal pheasants and hares, and sat on the Bench in judgement of those who transgressed them. A farm worker rarely ate meat, although a generous squire might bestow a couple of rabbits at Christmas.

Both labourer and tenant farmer worked in fields where the sacred game abounded and such temptation was often too much for them. It was a Norfolk tenant farmer who, tired of growing crops to be eaten down by his master's game, said as he blew out his brains, 'I die, but the rabbits have killed me.' A snare could be set while a man trimmed hedges, or he could slip from his cottage door after dark and take a pheasant by any one of a number of means from where they roosted, bulky and easy targets, in the thorn hedges. From a blend of bravado and necessity some took to the poaching life with a vengeance and, having no regular employment, became expert with the long net, massed ranks of snares or

'sniggles', and went in for wholesale slaughter of roosting game with gun or trail net. Few of them seemed to profit from their ill-gotten gains and tended to drink the profits in the alehouse.

The gamekeeper was no more wealthy than the poacher, but he was paid to protect his master's game and if this meant night-watching, being prepared to fight with his fists or a cudgel and risk his life to that end, then so be it. There were many desperate affrays in moonlit woodlands as the pages which follow will show.

The poacher has always been a hard bird to categorise. He could be a hungry cottager snatching a dinner for his family, or the professional moucher who sold his bag; but it was a county squire, and a JP to boot, who kept a catapult in his pocket and could not resist a shot at a pheasant in his neighbour's stubble. One of the greatest angling writers of all times shot for the pot in hard times during the war; a country parson kept an air rifle under the seat of his Morris Minor; and a schoolmaster appeared before the beak for shooting a pheasant (the property of a friend of his) from his car window. Colonel Peter Hawker, the father of English wildfowling and noted Hampshire squire, loved nothing better than to round up his friends and systematically shoot the coverts of his hated neighbour, the parson.

Further along the road of iniquity stood the likes of the late Kenzie Thorpe, one of the greatest wildfowlers of all time, latterly a respected naturalist, artist and companion of the wise and great, who had made a full and unashamed living as a poacher, making free with the royal preserves at the Sandringham estate and serving time in Norwich prison for one of his more extravagant exploits. There are many others of that mould, and they and keepers have waged an age-old war, first one and then the other gaining ascendancy but having always a grudging respect one for another and playing the game by unwritten rules. A few wished to challenge what they saw to be an unjust authority and archaic laws, while violent gangs came from the towns with the intention of clearing a man's coverts for profit. Each was different and yet all may be loosely bundled together under the all-embracing epithet, poacher.

In early days the penalty for capture was severe. Young lads – the 'King of the Norfolk Poachers', for example, at the age of twelve – were sent to jail for taking a rabbit; in earlier times the threat of transportation, and the horrors of the man trap and spring gun, were occupational hazards. Even those cruel deterrents could not stamp out the game, and here is the pith of it; poaching was in the bloodstream of some folk, as impossible to eradicate as to change the colour of their eyes.

There is another man, however, who does not earn the right to the name of poacher. He is idle, unemployed and unemployable. He shoots every bird a keeper has in order to sell it to the game dealer or at the back doors of hotels for what he can get for beer money. He sleeps by day while the keeper works, the same keeper who is on night-watch under the cold stars, clutching a pickaxe handle for comfort – a cold comfort indeed in such a frail stick of wood. This man, provided the odds were heavily in his favour, would think nothing of attacking a keeper

who was brave enough to accost him, a vicious assault leaving the victim broken and bleeding and in some cases dead.

Of the countryside and its arts, of the very real skills of the true poacher they are ignorant; back-street thugs who recognise a quick profit from a venture into the woods is all they are. They will poison a salmon river and shoot at bailiffs, strip a game cover and, mob-handed, care not who stands in their way. Beyond the pale of any civilised intercourse or consideration I wish them ill; doubtless it was those to whom my well-meaning advisers were referring when they expressed doubts as to the wisdom of a poaching book.

Have no fear: this book is not for the likes of them or their benighted souls. This book is of the lore, humour, country skills and diamond-cut diamond encounters between keepers and poachers, all of which have existed since the first Norman squire or medieval monarch paid a man to protect his game from others who desired to possess it. That battle continues, and will do so as long as birds, beasts and fish, those volatile and freest of spirits, are deemed to be the possessions of one man rather than another.

BEWARE
OLD VELVETEENS

The gamekeeper was there to protect his master's game from enemies of the two- and four-legged sort. In olden times he sprang from the same village stock as his arch-enemy the poacher. The local moucher who used the ancient arts to take game was a man the keeper could understand and he seemed at times almost to enjoy the cut-and-thrust, the diamond-cut-diamond of the age-old battle.

A good keeper was less easy to poach than was an idler, but sometimes he met his match; now and then fisticuffs were resorted to while cudgels swung and clunked on pates in the moonlit aisles of the woods. The keeper kept himself to himself and his real friends were few; his velveteen suit proclaimed his calling, and he was a feared and respected man in the community. He enjoyed the patronage and protection of his powerful employer and the retributive engine of the Game Laws. The odds in the poaching war were in his favour.

The Victorian Poacher

Gilbertson and Page used to make gamekeeping aids for the royal estates, one of the first firms to do so. Their products included all manner of game-rearing equipment, cures for gapes ('The Certain and Complete Cure'), a patent warm-water box for transferring young pheasants from hatching box to coop, game food, duck meal, dog biscuits and so on. Today they concentrate on the manufacture of dog food, their Valumix brand name being well known among gundog owners and trainers. In the heady days of the 1890s, when vanloads of keepering equipment left the firm each day and reared pheasants were in their heyday, they published a handy little manual for keepers warning them of telltale signs of poachers at work and how to combat them.

It was entitled *Poachers versus Keepers, an amusing and instructive treatise concerning poachers and their artifices – dealing with the many phases of poaching directed against game both fur and feathered* (they went in for wordy titles in those times) and priced at 6d (or about 2p modern equivalent). This is a very rare book in its original form, and it contains jewels of wisdom and wit.

The Keeper As A Detective

Unlike the policeman, the keeper cannot rely on the evidence of an aggrieved party but must use his eyes and ears to detect poaching. He is on his own. He must use all the fieldcraft of a plains Indian and be sharp-eyed to notice torn-up earth, a barked twig, tracks in the morning dew, or black footmarks on frosted herbage, all of which indicate that an intruder had been visiting at night. In those days the keepers were oft abroad and not confined to the rearing shed or seat of the Land-rover as many are today.

Like the observant Sherlock Holmes, a keeper can tell much from a few bent twigs and a fragment of wood, which would be hidden to the eye of an amateur. Such signs tell him that a hare has been snared in that run – the fresh-bitten bark is a giveaway; and the twig is a pricker dropped by the poacher – it is new and fresh-cut, otherwise it would have been polished from the friction of a pocket lining. This is therefore not the work of a practised old hand but of a less experienced chap, probably a local, a loafing labourer engaged on farm work or road mending.

A search down the hedge reveals an ash tree where the stick was cut, and even the whittlings in the ground, fresh and dry, which show it was the work of last night. But see, there is another

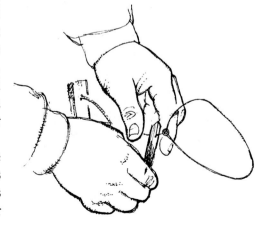

stub, white and fresh-cut, so another snare has been set. The good keeper hunts the fence and finds the place of the second snare, but this one has drawn a blank and what is more, the string holding the snare in place has been cut, so the poacher was disturbed and left in a hurry.

A further search of the ground reveals footprints. In the days of nail-shod boots this was as good as a fingerprint, for invariably there is a nail or two missing; the keeper notes this carefully and observes that the man tends to stand with his right foot pointing outwards. He takes the string home and compares it with a row of others he has found and matches them. The new one is not tied with the practised skill of the ones from the hand of a noted local poacher whom he has yet to catch red-handed, so the newcomer is a young chap with a crude notion of how to set a wire but with access to an expert who supplies him with proper snares.

So much from a little broken ground and some scuffed bark, which anyone else would pass by without a second glance. It so happens that our observant keeper recalls that the old hand well known to him associates with a young chap known to history as 'Artful'. The keeper seeks him out and engages him in conversation; he notices that his right foot has a tendency to turn outwards, and by the simple subterfuge of leading him over a muddy track, he can confirm that the boot has the same nails missing from its sole. Thus is 'Artful' identified, and it will be but a matter of time before he is nabbed.

OBSERVATION

The keeper will have his eyes peeled all the time, looking in the muddy gateways for signs of footprints and disturbed grass on the edge of the cornfield. Tobacco smoke is detectable a long way off and a keeper would not be averse to leaving a lump of smouldering baccy near a spot where he suspected intruders. The poacher would catch a whiff of tobacco on the breeze and make good his escape, laughing at the keeper for his clumsiness.

The keeper would be alert for bird movements, the harsh rattle of a jay warning of intruders, the clatter of pigeons leaving a distant stand of ash; something was disturbing those birds and he would not rest until he knew what it was. Blackbirds are also good guardians of woods and will always shriek their alarm at an intruder. Guinea fowl or geese could be kept in pens – these are probably the best guards of all.

A good keeper had a telescope or pair of binoculars to hand, not only to spy on intruders from afar but to note the resting places of the coveys at night, the movement of hares on the short stubbles and all manner of things useful to his job.

THE KEEPER AND THE LOCALS

A good keeper appeared to be friends with one and all, but such was only his deviousness. In fact he trusted nobody and had few if any friends outside his own profession. A wise keeper showed friendliness to the locals, and so got to recognise the characters and hoped by his manner to lull them into a false sense of security. He might establish a 'mole' who would keep him informed of nefarious goings-on: this man would be rewarded with small cash sums and all meetings with him would be secret in case he blew his cover.

Such a keeper would be near the roads late at night, watching who came home from work late, who slipped out of the pub before closing time for no apparent reason, and what itinerant labourers were working in the area. In this way he knew who was where at what time, and was the better able to spot someone acting suspiciously. When approaching someone working in the fields the keeper never took a direct route but retreated and approached from an unlikely direction the better to catch folk off their guard and maybe overhear some careless conversation before they knew he was there. In addition, his habit of popping up out of the blue at unexpected times made folk feel uneasy, never quite sure where he would appear next; this was all to the keeper's advantage.

In conversation the keeper would sham tiredness, as a man who was abroad at all hours. He might remark at how light it was still at midnight last night, and mention in passing the sharp rainstorm which fell at 2am. In this way word would spread like wildfire of what a vigilant man he was, never sleeping and always out on watch. This did his reputation no harm.

KEEPER IN DRAG

Many a criminal has escaped arrest due to no more than the shiny buttons on a policeman's tunic; they betray his presence as a ray of light catches them. For this reason some keepers were averse to the showy livery which became customary on some great shoots at the turn of the century. Such garb stood out a mile away and acted as a flag of warning to potential wrongdoers. A wise keeper persuaded his employer to allow him to wear fustian about his daily duties and keep his smart livery for the shooting day only.

Sometimes a keeper would go further and assume a disguise to throw the poacher off the scent. One especially inventive man disguised himself variously as a peasant in a smock, a priest in a felt hat and frock coat, a soldier in uniform, and once as a woman selling apples. He even went to the lengths of shaving off his luxuriant beard, the better to throw suspicious folk off the scent – even in those days bearded lady apple sellers could not have been that thick on the ground.

NIGHT-POACHING

Night-poaching was the hardest of all to eradicate. The only remedy was constant watching, changing places, acting on information received, and the keeper doing his best to anticipate the next move. Night-watching was described as the curse of the keeper's life, but he had to do it, and he also had to be on parade on his usual rounds in the day-time, so in the winter he could get little sleep. Even when he assured himself that all was well and that he might safely go home and snatch a few hours well-deserved sleep, the gang would be out with their nets sweeping his stubbles; for their information was usually better than his, they being many and he but one.

THE ALARM GUN

This was one recommended answer. The gun was set by a footpath and the wire stretched across it at a distance from the ground high enough to be avoided by a passing hare or fox. The sudden explosion had the double effect of startling the poacher and sending him running off and also of alerting game in the area that danger was afoot. At the sound of the shot rabbits would scuttle to their buries and hares sneak into the next field.

The experienced poacher would feel his way cautiously along a ride, groping like a blind man with a twig or reed for any wire set across the path. When he came across one he would snip it and thus disarm the gun. A cool customer would not dash away in panic at the sound of the gun going off, but lie in wait to make sure someone was coming. If the gun had not done its job and given the alarm, he would continue on his way.

The keeper would fix a counter-weight on the gun and set the trigger very fine so that even with the wire cut the gun would still detonate. Alternatively he would set the wire at chest height, or he would vary it, so that the probing cane of the poacher would miss it. A more sophisticated response was the double alarm gun. On hearing the first shot, all unexpected as it was, the watchers often had a job to pinpoint the exact location of the sound, especially on an estate where a great number of guns were set. The double gun was designed to go off some fifteen seconds after the trip wire was broken; the first shot aroused the keeper and set him alert, the second allowed him to calculate precisely whence the sound had come.

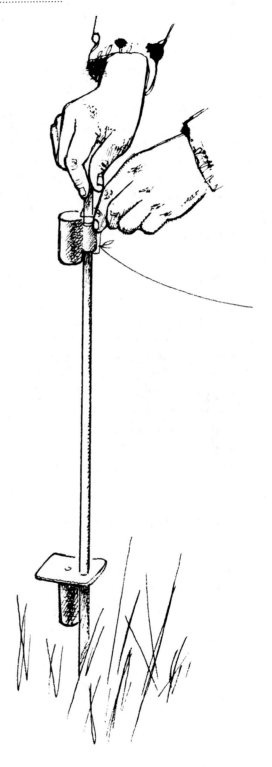

The Shepherd Bagged

A shepherd lived in a cottage adjoining a barn on the outskirts of the village. His kitchen garden held a splendid array of greenstuffs which stood well into the winter and which he never seemed to cut for cooking. The alert keeper suspected that the greens were left solely to attract game which the shepherd was culling at his convenience.

Calling by the cottage, the keeper saw two small boys playing in the garden. 'Ever see any bunnies in the garden, Tommy?'

'Yes sir; they be here often; my daddy ties 'em up in the hedge.' Fools, drunkards and children usually speak the truth, so he examined the hedge and saw a well-worn hare run which had been disguised with thorns. He decided on a night watch, and creeping back later with one of the other keepers, saw that the thorns had been removed and a snare left in the gap.

They hid in the wood nearby, hoping to catch the shepherd red-handed removing a hare from the snare. After some hours the squeal of a hare broke the silence, for one had run into the wire. The keepers were confident that the poacher would appear to remove his catch – but not so. 'I wonder why he doesn't fetch her', shivered one.

After a while they made a cautious survey and found that the hare had vanished along with the snare; and yet no man had been seen, that they would swear to. Exactly the same occurred two nights later, at which point the head keeper himself made a closer examination of the wire. He discovered a hidden cord which ran from the snare straight up to the shepherd's bedroom window; the old rascal hauled the hare up to his window – which explained the sudden squealing followed by the inexplicable silence.

The head keeper sent his man home to fetch a hare from the game larder; they put it into the snare and gave a passable imitation of the hare's squeal of distress. Sure enough, the cord tightened but this time met an unexpected resistance. There came a muffled voice from above: 'The old bugger's caught up on the fence; I shall have to go an fetch her!'

The shepherd emerged in his nightgown with no slippers and crept down his garden where he was duly collared. The keepers would not allow him go back inside and get dressed, but frog-marched him as he was – all but naked – over four large fields to the keeper's house. There he was given a worn suit of velveteens and locked up on the charge of night-poaching.

The shepherd had not rigged up the string retrieval system to avoid capture, but only to avoid having to leave his warm bedroom in the chill of the winter's night.

THE TAR BABY

A certain keeper was suffering great annoyance from a solitary poacher. Often he would hear the sound of shots in his woods but no matter how quickly he was at the spot, the poacher had made good his escape. The keeper was single-handed and had no-one to help him watch, and a man has to sleep sometime. However, the shooting season was approaching and at last he hit on a likely way of catching his tormentor.

On every latch on every gate in his woods he set a small stone, so that anyone going through needs must dislodge them – then he would at least know the route used by his adversary. That night there was the sound of shots but the keeper stayed safe in bed, secure in the knowledge that his man was as good as caught. But to his surprise next day he found that not one of his stones had been dislodged; obviously the poacher kept clear of potential danger points.

Next the keeper marked all the gaps and stiles, placing a tuft of grass on the

top of each stile so that anyone crossing could not avoid knocking them down, and he drew a thin briar across every gap in the fences and hedges. The next morning a dislodged tuft showed the track the poacher used to enter the wood. The keeper needed no more information, but set about the digging of a huge pit some six feet across and nine deep. It was a whole day of heavy labour but he felt the effort to be worth it. The going was easy enough, being for the most part sand. The spoil he wheeled away on a barrow and hid.

The pit looked a formidable obstacle when complete, but the keeper's feeling was that it would not be enough simply to send the poacher crashing down to the bottom, possibly firing his gun as he did so. His instinct was to cover the bottom of his trap with pointed stakes, though in the end his Christian feelings caused him to abandon this drastic punishment. Instead he filled the bottom of the pit with tar. He had a good supply at home in readiness for fuming out rabbits, and he supplemented this with a fresh barrel bought from the local gas works.

The hole he lovingly covered with rotten twigs, bark, moss and dry grass, and in the end he would have defied the sharpest eye to have spotted its presence; and he was further comforted by the reflection that the poacher would be walking the track under cover of darkness. He took pleasure from the picture of the man wandering along gazing upwards for roosting pheasants and then plunging down to his doom.

The trap worked with spectacular success. Eagerly the keeper hurried down next day, to see that the unlucky victim had fallen his length into the pit, firing his gun as he crashed down, but presumably without injuring himself, for the man had climbed out, although the keeper was puzzled to think how he could have done so, leaving his gun in the path and plentiful tracks of black footprints and finger marks on every gate and stile as he made his way home.

Suddenly it was noted by all in the village that a certain individual had retired from circulation and was not to be found in his usual haunts. At the same time the demand for soap in that particular house became enormous, special preference being for the especially strong Monkey Brand. This utterly astonished the village shopkeeper, for the family hitherto had not expressed much interest in cleanliness, as the grimy faces of the children made all too clear. The reason for this sudden desire for soap was a mystery to all save the keeper.

Often afterwards he would be sitting in his cottage and would break into a chuckle at the remembrance of his own particular piece of cleverness. 'What be you a-larfin' at?' queried his missus. 'Do you ever hear any shots in the woods now a' nights?' 'No,' says the missus. 'Well, that's what I'm a-larfin' at.'

THE WHISTLE

The old-fashioned police whistle was a favourite communication system of keepers. Today they are armed with two-way radios, but in Victorian times there was no such thing. The shrill sound carried great distances and by a series of different calls the keepers could pass messages to each other. Also, a number of whistles blown from different places made it quite clear to the poachers that the keeper was not alone, and might make them think twice before they launched a cowardly attack on what they would have preferred to have been one man alone. Psychologically the police whistle had a great advantage, just as a siren has today.

IN THE BAG

Some night poachers were more desperate, and would come armed to the teeth with the sole intention of raiding a keeper's coverts, making no pretence at secrecy and more than ready to show fight if approached. The lone keeper was warned on no account to approach such a fearful gang, and only to face up to them if his numbers equalled or exceeded theirs. The only good advice was to stay clear, possibly bag small groups of the gang as they made their way home separately by different paths, or to get them after they had sobered up: poaching gangs were usually the worse for drink and all the more dangerous for it.

One ingenious keeper managed to defeat a large gang. When on night watch he heard the sound of many footfalls crunching on the fallen leaves. From his hiding place he counted thirteen poachers, well armed and purposeful, walking in Indian file along the ride. None of them was known to him and he realised that it would be madness for him to tackle them alone; but he was a determined man, and keen to save his master's game.

He raised his voice in a loud alarm call, then again in a lower tone, cheered at several pitches of his voice and interspersed it with view halloos, crashing about in the bushes the while in an attempt to represent a veritable army of keepers and

I am deeply indebted to the retired keeper Mr James Knight of Yeovil, Somerset, who sent me many pages of priceless reminiscences and views, all carefully written in a copperplate hand and recalling a depth of wisdom and country lore of which even Richard Jefferies would not have been ashamed. I use his words as follows.

SIGNS OF TROUBLE

Cattle and horses with pricked ears watching in the same direction.
Pigeons clattering out of a wood or hedgerow.
Hare at speed yet stopping to look back, then away again.
Only the odd rabbit instead of several, uneasy near hedge or wood.
Carrion crows voicing and leaving cover.
Deer on the move, stopping often to look back.
Mud left on the gate top by a boot being dragged over.
Dew, cobwebs, frost, mud and twigs all leave signs.
Pigeons and crows jinking in flight and turning back.
Birdsong cut short and magpie chatter.
Early morning village dogs barking.
Parked vehicles early and late.
The various alarms of blackbirds and wrens.

The good poacher always reads nature before a sortie: the good keeper should also learn from these signs.

FIELDCRAFT

I was once called out to help a keeper on an estate; the poachers were there, it was certain, and everyone was on the lookout. By 9 o'clock most were called away to their jobs, but I and three keepers hung on. Within half an hour I said, 'I know where your poachers are. You two slowly walk and make for that distant tree, the other keeper come with me.'

We came in from behind and caught them in a hedgerow in a snug, well-used hide, put where they could see and not be seen. Sheer woodcraft on their part, but mine was better: I knew where they were after the second pigeon had jinked above them. One keeper remarked 'I should never have thought of that': educated, yes, also smart and well spoken – but sons of the soil ... No!

police. The echoes of the woods aided his deception and to his delight the poachers broke up in disarray and made off in panic in all directions. One of them actually stumbled on the keeper's prostrate form as he hid in the bushes and he gave the man a good thrashing before arresting him. The general confusion caused by the poachers' flight added to the illusion that an army was come upon them.

GYPSIES

The Victorian keeper had little time for gypsies with their packs of lurcher dogs and cunning ways. They were as versed in the ways of the countryside as was he. Their womenfolk would call at his house with some paltry excuse such as selling clothes pegs, but really to establish whether or not he was at home. The men would set wires close to their caravans and snatch them up quickly when the keeper appeared. Their rough dogs would range the countryside not only snapping up hares and rabbits but causing great disturbance to the game covers.

Even the allotment holder was one to be watched. A cunning gardener was not averse to allowing some winter greens to grow thickly near his boundary, knowing well that hares would be attracted to them in winter when the snow lay thick. Rabbits would burrow into his carrot clamp, and the gardener who tended to work his ground early in the morning and late at night was worth watching. A wise keeper would chat to the man on some pretext or other and allow his dogs to run through the vegetable plot so that any game sheltering there would be disturbed.

'A SNAPPER-UP OF UNCONSIDERED TRIFLES'

It is impossible to debate the character of 'the average poacher' for there ain't no such animal. Some were born to it, others took to it from necessity, as a means of striking a blow at authority, and some poached for pure devilment. No doubt a few felt a sense of injustice that game birds and animals which were free to come and go could be owned by one person who passed ferocious laws to assert that privilege, and who himself sat on the Bench to sentence those who transgressed.

The majority did not harbour such high falutin', politically luxurious thoughts, but poached to fill their bellies, for the sport of it, the adventure and the risk. The money they earned in this hard way was more often than not squandered in the pub.

QUALITIES OF THE POACHER

To be a good Victorian poacher the experts felt you needed to be a sharp-witted fellow, and that at least is true today. The poacher must have a good knowledge of the animals and birds he pursues, and have extraordinary patience, and be resilient to all the counter-measures of his old enemy the gamekeeper. He must be a good judge of weather and know that full moon favours midnight shooting, that rough, windy weather with dark nights is best for trail-netting, and that foggy weather is best for slipping secretly into forbidden woods and indulging in a little ferreting. He knows, too, that hard frost is all but useless, for a man cannot even drive a snare peg into the ground in such conditions.

By tradition a poor gardener and idle farm labourer, he will sit making nets for hours upon end, a task from which he believes he will reap direct benefit, unlike slogging away for someone else. Sentimentalists view him with warmth, the hero of songs such as *The Lincolnshire Poacher,* that Robin Hood figure who resists brutal tyranny and the injustices of the Game Laws and catches game to feed a starving family in a tied cottage. Gilbertson and Page would have us believe that in reality the poacher was a 'sullen wretch ... his days spent in drinking in company with his ribald companions and his nights in breaking the laws. Rarely indeed are his illicit gains of any benefit to him; he is obliged to sell the game at a price far below market value and the proceeds go to swell the alehouse coffers'. In fact, a man who spent all his days in the pub with no visible means of support was one who merited close watch by a keeper, for he could well be coming by his beer money by nefarious, nocturnal activities.

KNOWING YOUR PLACE

In times past, small children at school would chant the hymn about 'The rich man in his castle, the poor man at his gate, God made them high or lowly, and ordered their estate'. Poaching was represented to them as a great evil, the first step on a downward path to everlasting damnation: from his privileged position in the pulpit, the parson would wax thunderous about the squire's pheasants: 'Constant participation in petty crime will soon blunt the slender perception of right which a man previously possessed; drink and ribald company add to the evil, and he eventually becomes a confirmed criminal regarding all guardians of property as his natural enemies'. Heavy stuff for a man who would supplement his diet of turnips with one of the squire's hares, for hares and rabbits generally were preferred to pheasants by village poachers; you could feed a large family on a hare, and it was easier to catch.

As for motive, the moralists of the last century made a fine discernment between the poacher who shot a pheasant in a tree and the squire who brought one down as it flew over him on a shooting day. The poacher was only very slightly motivated by a desire for sport and excitement; he had more pleasure from pocketing a hare than from seeing how many times his dog turned it, and for him the bottom line was the few shillings he might earn from his ill-gotten gains. This view would certainly be contested by some modern poachers. Kenzie Thorpe summed it up thus: 'It's the sport man; it's the sport!'

THE POACHING FAMILY

Then as now, poaching tended to run in the blood of certain families, from the youngest to the oldest and stretching back many generations. Hearing nothing but poaching yarns and tricks from their mother's knee, it is not surprising they were more than willing to join in at the earliest opportunity what was represented to them as exciting adventures and hairbreadth escapes. They were taught the underlying principle that game was the rightful spoil of anyone who could take it.

CHILDREN POACHERS

Such children were not long waiting for an apprenticeship. The traditional first employment as bird-starver at a penny a day gave legitimate access to the fields and preserved ground. Their sharp eyes could spot a sitting bird and a hare track more quickly than most. They could hide their small persons in the tiniest nook, and whistle or sing a warning of approaching officialdom as well as an adult and with less chance of arousing suspicion.

The Victorian moralist was at pains to point out the hardships of poaching. As well as being damned to eternal fires, the poacher was likely to be often unwell as a result of exposure to all weathers, irregular meals, lack of sleep and excessive drinking, usually of 'ardent liquors'. He was regarded by respectable folk as an outlaw and generally mistrusted and shunned; although admired by a very few who envied his disrespect for the law but dared not follow his example.

THE POACHER'S WOMAN

The poacher's wife was a subject of sympathy, for the only time she saw her husband he was likely to be drunk, and of course he was out at night about his business. She found what money she could by going through his pockets when he was incapable, and more often than not was buffeted for her pains when the good man discovered his loss. When he failed to return home it was not for the common reason of being with another woman but because the keepers had bagged him and marched him off to gaol. At least the wife had the comfort of knowing where he was and that he could do no harm, and rather preferred life with her man in gaol than out of it.

She dreaded his return, for not only would he be as surly as before, but he would now be a man with a grudge – and she could but guess and fear at how he would seek redress for his punishment.

The First Offender

No poacher ever caught admitted that the case in question was anything more than his first offence. An obviously hardened veteran would be taken into custody bewailing the fact that it was '...the first time I've ever poached'. The desk sergeant would probably observe with ill-concealed sarcasm how fortunate it was that so many miscreants were bagged on their very first outing; the keepers were to be heartily congratulated that they kept poaching to such a low level by nailing every poacher his first time out.

The Poacher as a Helper

Sometimes the locals were called out to help with the Hunt or to beat on formal shooting days. This was also a source of irritation to keepers, for again this gave the rogues free access to the prime woods and they would surely be making plans for midnight raids when the leaf was off the trees.

With all the benefits of broad daylight and a legitimate reason for his being there, the poacher will make careful note of hare runs through fences; in a quiet

moment he will slip into the coverts and see where the keeper feeds the birds and note, by the piles of droppings, the trees the pheasants prefer for roosting. On a shooting day a poacher must be watched at all times, and ought not to be entrusted with carrying any birds back to the cart unless one or two are not to go mysteriously missing. The only comfort which the keeper can seek is that at least the man is under his eye at such times – for it is unseen that the poacher is at his most dangerous.

A party of keepers made it a custom to spend their shooting tips on a glorious booze-up in the village pub at the end of a shooting day. They were entitled to relax after their efforts and they deserved at least one good carouse. The beaters, however, being well aware of this, would spend the day hiding various items of game behind bushes, under a tall tree or in a culvert. A pheasant might easily slip from the hand of a man overburdened with birds and should the keeper notice it, he can but say 'Bless my soul!' (or words to that effect), 'I didn't know I'd dropped it'.

And when the keepers made merry later in the evening, a few shadowy figures could be seen collecting the booty from where it had been cached; but of course, there was never anyone in authority there to see them. A good poacher will always be one jump ahead of a keeper who makes the mistake of falling into set ways and habits which make him vulnerable.

THE FARM LABOURER

The hardest poacher to bring to book was the farm worker. He had a legitimate reason to be on and about the land, and even the most vigilant keeper could not keep watch on him all day. It is an easy matter for a man in the fields to set a snare and keep half an eye on it as he works with scythe or pitchfork. A telltale sign was the man who spent his lunch-hour wandering about 'just to keep myself warm', when anyone with any sense would have been resting under the hedge, having been on his feet for six hours. The wanderer was looking at the dyke edges and hedge bottoms for signs of rabbit and hare runs.

Another chap to watch was the one who left his work after his mates had departed. Leaving early one could understand, but the man who lingered after everyone else had gone whistling and talking down the lane had a reason for doing so, and it was not a pure love of hard work. It was more than likely that he would be checking snares and traps set earlier in the day, things he would not care to do with onlookers.

A poaching labourer would not be averse to stealing a vermin trap set by the keeper, so these should be kept well hidden and away from fields in which work was taking place during the day. A wise keeper marked his traps by filing a small notch on each one, insignificant to all eyes but his own, so that he could identify it should he miss it, and find it craftily set in another place by the person who had stolen it.

Even the innocent bird-scarer at a penny a day was worth keeping a beady eye on, especially one to whom the farmer had loaned an old muzzle-loader to help

him with his work. Only a very foolish farmer indeed would allow shot to be taken onto the field, but should issue only powder. Shot would be pointless as the lad would be such an execrable marksman that he could never hit a flying rook or, indeed, a flying anything, while sitting rooks were, and are, far too cunning to allow him to creep within range. However, a cunning lad could use substitutes – a handful of iron-hard wheat, homemade shot, tin-tacks or even small stones were more than sufficient to rake a covey at close quarters, shoot a pheasant in a tree or a hare in a form.

A good keeper would be able to differentiate between the distant sound of a shot from a gun fully charged and one loaded with powder only. If in doubt the keeper had only to engage the lad in conversation, ask to look at his gun, duly admire it and then 'accidentally' discharge it into the ground. He would know instantly by the recoil and by the hole blown in the stubble if the gun was loaded with shot, in which case he knew just what to do with the unlucky lad. If the gun was innocently loaded with powder only, he would curse his clumsiness and apologise for wasting the charge.

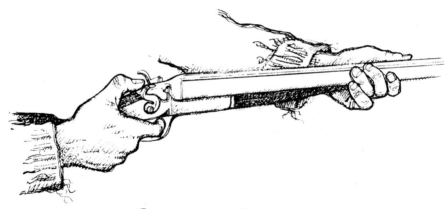

OUT OF THE MOUTHS

One crafty labourer could not resist the sight of so many hares and rabbits playing near his cottage when he and his family knew not the taste of meat. His custom was to set snares within sight of his house and when he made a catch he would send out his children to play.

In all innocence one of them would happen on the rabbit in a wire and would rush home with it to his mother – as any child would – without the cottager in any way being implicated. On one occasion the lad was fairly caught, but in the face of a rigorous cross-examination pleaded all innocence: 'I found it when I was playing, and was taking it home to my mammy' was all he would say. When taken to his father, the man vigorously denied any involvement and suggested the keepers lock up the small miscreant.

Of course they had to let him go, and wait for a more clear-cut opportunity. The keepers were extra diligent in their watching and at last were rewarded in fairly catching the man in the act of setting a wire.

The Death of 'Blucher'

Letter to the Shooting Times *1905*

Latimore Lee, or to call him by his nickname, 'Blucher' – the notorious Lincolnshire poacher has been run to ground for the last time. A few days ago Death came to the keepers' aid and grimly and tragically laid his hands on 'Blucher' when he was in the very act of following his lawless avocation.

The old man – he was over 60 years of age – left his home with a comrade, to all appearances, for an aimless walk in the fields which he loved so dearly. But on his way, entering a dilapidated hovel, he took a gunstock and a barrel from a hiding place under some hay. 'Blucher' it seems, had made up his mind to try and get a rabbit for the following day's dinner. He secreted the stock in one trouser leg and the barrel and ramrod in the other.

Then, a few minutes later as the men were approaching some coverts near Barrowby, with appalling suddenness there came a report, and he reeled to earth with a gaping wound in his side. The poacher's faithful dog, 'the silent dog' as he was generally known, lay down by the dying man's side. His friend covered 'Blucher' with an overcoat and then quickly, and weeping, hurried in to Grantham and informed the Police of the accident.

Apart from his record of over 50 convictions for poaching, Lee was known the county over as an absolutely honest and upright man. An incident characteristic of him is worth relating. He was seen one morning coming down one of the streets on the outskirts of Grantham and in company with him, a man who had a bag of onions on his back. A constable met the pair and promptly took them into custody.

'Blucher' was charged jointly with the other man with theft. The old man's look and speech to the bench convinced them of his innocence. 'Stealing onions!' he gasped; 'Why, I'd scorn to do such a thing. You know what my business is, it's only poaching.'

Blucher's dog instinctively knew when danger was ahead and would go quietly up to his master and lay his nose in his open hand.

'HOVERER' ON WOMEN POACHERS; 1907

Women are rarely found actually poaching, but more frequently as confederates and accessories after or before the fact, as legal gentlemen say. For this they are very well adapted, both physically and because of their wit. A keen woman may be of the greatest use to a poacher, and if she is given to babbling and too sharp on his behalf, a veritable danger. A woman's tongue has brought many a criminal well-merited punishment and a very simple action on the part of the poacher's wife may prove her husband's undoing.

A poacher's wet clothes hung on a garden fence to dry after he has returned from his nightly excursions and retired to rest has placed many a keeper in possession of the man's real profession and caused him to be closely watched until captured. The sale of a hare skin to a supposed peddler has also given the game away. More than one poacher has suffered 'three week's hard' because of his wife's yearning for the threepence a hare skin realises.

As before stated, it is as confederates to poaching that women shine, for they are able to penetrate anywhere in search of information. An old woman will venture into the most sacred covert, avowedly in search of sticks for the fire, or some other errand for she is nothing if not ready with an excuse when necessary. She will carry nets, snares or a gun through the area upon which a suspected man bearing either would be searched. Her clothing is far more adapted than that of a man to the concealment of such material.

'All the world loves a lover', and who would suspect a courting couple resting on a stile of having designs against the game? However, the courting couple may be but a blind, and, perhaps, if the pair are watched, the girl will be found sitting alone while her swain sets snares close by. Many a young poacher, afraid that his nightly excursions from the village just after dark would attract attention, has sauntered forth with a girl on his arm and she has returned home later. There are indeed many ways in which women are able to assist poachers without actually sharing their work.

SHOOTING TIMES, 1897

For all his boasting and occasional serious crimes, the poacher cannot be said to possess great courage. He will put up a very good fight sometimes, but that only occurs when it is the way of escaping arrest. Under such conditions he has been know to fight severely, but it is a conflict of desperation not of courage. The average poacher is full of nerves and it would be hard to find one who will not take freely to his legs if by that means lies the slightest chance of getting away. Once the risk of losing liberty confronts a poacher he is transformed either into a supreme coward or a desperate maniac, and it is the latter condition which is responsible for the serious affrays which occasionally startle society and give rise to ideas that such crimes would be better prevented by rendering the preservation of game impossible.

One day last Winter we visited with a keeper a well stocked rabbit warren. During the season a night never passes that alarm guns are not set in this warren and another favourite precaution is barbed wire extended at a height of a foot from the ground. The night previous a poacher had evidently sprung one of the guns, and imagining he had been shot at, dashed away in fright. He was intercepted by the wire and, judging from the remnants of clothing attached thereto, had suffered an experience likely to do more good in preventing further attempts at poaching than half a dozen small fines.

A keeper's ingenuity is supposed to stop at sawing a plank half through when he wishes to play a trick on the poacher and immerse him in the brook running beneath, but a poacher we know would hardly agree to that infertility of resource.

He was seeking a pheasant at roost to shoot it, when the contents of a bucket of tar were emptied all over him, being dislodged by a wire touched beneath. The keeper tracked him to his home by the drippings of tar and smears on gates and stiles and, instead of prosecuting, added insult to injury by sending him a pound of tallow.

From The Amateur Poacher *by Richard Jefferies*

OBY'S ADVICE

'All as I can tell you of the dodge is this: you watch everybody, and be always in the fields and always work one parish till you knows every hare in un, and always work by yourself and don't have no mates.'

OBY'S THEORY

'The reason I gets on so well poaching is because I'm always at work out in the fields, except when I goes with the van. I watches everything that goes on, and marks the hare's tracks and the rabbit buries, and the double mounds and little copses as the pheasants wander off to in the Autumn. I keeps a nation good lookout after the keeper and his men, and sees their dodges – which way they walks and how they comes back sudden and unexpected on purpose. There's mostly one about with his eyes on me – when they see me working on a farm they puts a man special to look after me. I never does nothing close round where I'm at work, so he waits about a main bit for nothing.'

CIVILITY

John Wilkins was a Hertfordshire gamekeeper of the nineteenth century.
He had many run-ins with poachers during his long life.

Treat poachers as you would like to be treated yourself if you happened to be in their position, whether you catch them pheasant shooting at night or gate netting by day or poaching in any other way. Treat them as if they were men and not wild beasts for as you treat them, so they will treat you to a great extent.

If you hear them in the wood at night shooting, don't hide up behind a tree that you know they will pass by with your stick raised like a man with his bat at the wickets waiting for the ball and then as he passes knock him down before he sees you or you have spoken to him.

(Although a hard man, Wilkins took his own advice and often gave captured poachers money if they were down on their luck, saw to the wives and families of men in prison, and often took the lone poacher home with him for a bit of supper and a pipe before taking him to the magistrates. To one he gave a bushel of seed potatoes and to another a scythe. Many of them turned honest men as a result of his humanity, and also kept him informed of the proposed activities of their former associates if Wilkins or his estate were to be the target.)

HOW TO LOOK INNOCENT

Alfred Curtis was a poacher of the old school, using his skills to feed his family, never using violence, never taking more game than he needed, but a genuine, unsentimental countryman.

Often in late afternoon I would go off rabbiting and there would be Brinnie sitting on the cross bar of the bike where I had fixed a pad for him, forepaws on the handlebars. At times on the quiet road we would meet the village Policeman. He would give me a glance, catch sight of Brinnie sitting there and smile good naturedly. He saw nothing but a happy couple there together on the bike. If ever such a thought entered his head, well surely such a little dog as that could never catch a rabbit! In fact Brinnie could, but that was not the reason for her presence. Brinnie was there to drive the rabbits into the nets I should lay, and from the first rabbit I took from the net he would have the liver as a reward.

But there were other times when coming home I met the same Policeman and he showed suspicion. 'Hoi, just a minute!' Then I pretended not to have heard aright. 'Half-past four! Half-past four!' I would call out and pedal for all I was worth till far enough away or out of sight.

THE OLD POACHER

When I knew him he was getting old and he had crawled about so much in the damp undergrowth and crouched so long upon the moist earth that his knees were thickened and stiffened with rheumatism so that he would never run again. He came to cutting up pieces of carpet to make covers for his knees and finding that they were soon soaked with wet grasses, he begged some old inner tubes of tyres and made knee pads from those.

He thought nothing of going off into the woods for a week, living there without setting foot beyond, like a wild creature himself. He could move with no more noise than a cat; 'I'm a quiet man, myself,' he would say.

THREE POACHERS

From James Knight, retired Somerset keeper – words of wisdom which reveal a deep knowledge and love of country life.

Poachers ... there are three types: the genuine old 'sod', a part of the countryside, satisfied with the odd hare or bird, his interest being the humble rabbit, seldom carries a gun and never violent, knows as much about the estate as the keeper, if not more: can be helpful! Would make a first class keeper.

No 2, the misfits; usually work in gangs of two or three, no knowledge of woodcraft, carry guns and can be violent when cornered. The nuisance and unrest they cause outweighs their bag: easier to catch than No 1.

No 3, well planned, distance no problem. On Primrose Day, man, wife and little daughter on the estate picking flowers, but taking note of release pens, ditches, bridges, etc ... 'The Pathfinders; they are armed with something the keeper is not; they know when they are coming and the keeper don't. They are experts at their job.

The modern keeper is his own worst enemy; he has been taught to think like a keeper; you should think like a poacher and watch and woodcraft as a poacher. Get out and about *on foot* at unearthly hours, be seen by headlights in all sorts of places at all sorts of times; Word gets around. If I was a poacher and required a few salmon, an old sock with a stone in plus some Cymag is quick: if I required

44

some birds it would be on the roughest wet night we could get. I certainly wouldn't pick a moonlight, quiet night unless I wanted to be caught.

The Land Rover is the curse of the keeper; far too easy to drive around all day and night and not see anything worth seeing.

DEALING WITH POACHERS

If confronted by the village poacher I always come away a wiser man. He would never insult my intelligence by silly excuses; the only sorry part was that we were divided by the fence of the Law.

If confronted by two poachers with guns, the first thing to do is demand they unload same, then I unload mine. Sum up quietly if there is fight in them – usually not. If you sense that there is, act quick and fast: floor one, swing to the other and shout 'Do you want the same?' Usually, No! If confronted with three poachers I *must* have my back to a tree; three means there is likely to be trouble, and there may be a hiding coming your way. Boot into one, fist into another and the third often says, 'OK, I won't fight'. You must be quick to take advantage of surprise.

If there is four or more it's a bloody silly keeper who thinks a fight is the answer. Don't run away, pluck up courage and try to converse; get them on their way – there's always another day. But if you catch them with their loot that's a different matter. Shout; panic them by calling for other keepers (even if they don't exist), get them running with their swag – fire a shot in the air and they will drop some of it. Call: 'Jack, Bert, Bill!' and at seventy yards your damn gun accidentally fires low ... more booty dropped, and that is probably the last you see of them.

Mind you, I was 6ft 3in, 15 stone, and as good as they come.

THE ALTERNATIVE APPROACH

The only trusted friend I had in fifty years of keepering was a poacher. He was a member of a group of poachers I was after – first I just watched and waited, then at last I saw them cock a wire. Next morning before light I was in position ready for them to take this rabbit from the wire – I had put it there! When they did, I grabbed one man and said, 'How do you want it, rough or sensible?' They all agreed to be sensible. I arranged a meeting that evening; none of them were idiots, they knew all the tricks of their trade as their fathers were poachers long before them. They were part of the countryside.

After a good cussing I offered them a couple of rough hedges to ferret and the one field to wire; if they so much as looked into another field they were out, with my size 13 behind them. I was repaid tenfold. Any poachers in the area they knew of, and I would be warned when they were planning a raid. A couple even

The Fox Twins

The Fox twins, Albert Ebenezer and Ebenezer Albert, started the poaching game in Hertfordshire in 1871 with a stolen gun. In twenty years they amassed a spectacular total of 202 game law convictions, and the police had confiscated from them fifty guns. Their convictions would have numbered a good many more were it not for their standard defences when paraded before Hitchin magistrates' court. The one was mistaken identity (they were identical twins), and if this failed, the second was that they were out gathering mushrooms.

The Uses of Petticoats

Three Denbigh policemen were out in September 1887 when they saw two notorious poachers, Wynne and Gallimore, coming from the fields. They were thoroughly searched but were 'clean'.

Some time later three women belonging to the men were seen going to a spot in a neighbouring field, and appeared to be hiding something about their persons. They were detained and twenty-seven rabbits and two big nets were found on them. The women had tied the rabbits by the legs and slung them over stout bands fixed under their dresses. They were reluctant to part with their booty but were all prosecuted.

The then editor of *The Shooting Times*, Mr Lewis Clement, recalled how he had once caught a gypsy woman with seven or eight rabbits under her clothes. 'I tripped her up, as if by accident, and in her fall the rabbits were, of course, exposed to our gaze. She had obtained them by running a whippet in the warren.'

used to keep watch while I took a break; there was complete trust between us. One of them later in life became mayor in a small Berkshire town – none better. One ended up as a keeper and a damn good one; he never let me down. I learnt him the Euston system and the main facts of good keepering.

I took over a large shoot in Dorset, and one time I was hit and hit hard. I arrived too late to find my release pen a slaughterhouse – but although I remained on this shoot a further five years, I was never touched again. When I retired I was sitting on a seat one day down in the town, when a rough van with two rougher bearded men drew up. 'You're Mr Knight.' They said they were sorry to hear about my ill health, and said they were also sorry for the raid five years before. I asked them why they never came again. They said because their dogs were in the pen but I never shot them. 'We thank you and respect you for it. You said it's the owners to blame and not the dogs. Word was given to leave you alone.' Later I found out that it was the village poacher had told them that, and had asked them to give me a rest. It was certainly worth a couple of hedges of rabbits!

I used to know every damn twig on my shoot. Now I suppose today's keeper knows only the mpg and mph of his Land Rover, and feels he can deal with a bunch of idiots poaching his estate. Maybe he can, but I am talking about real poachers.

THE CONVERSION OF BUNNY AUSTIN

Within a week of moving to a new shoot I was warned to keep a sharp lookout for Bunny Austin, an out-and-out poacher whom no-one had ever caught. The next week in the evening I saw him from 500 yards come and set a few wires. I was there next morning with a rabbit which I put in his wire, and in its mouth I placed a cigarette packet on which I wrote 'Hello Bunny; turn round'. Sure enough he did: 'I suppose I'm in for it now'.

'Let's have a talk,' said I. He was small and thin and reminded me of a little owl. He stood still but his head was for ever turning, his beady eyes always watching. His main grumble was that although my boss was always complaining about rabbit damage, whenever he – Bunny – asked permission to catch them, he was told to 'get out and stay out' in no uncertain terms. I gave Bunny written permission to wire and ferret three or four fields and hedgerows, but no guns. He said he never used the bloody things – too noisy. I inspected his work each week and found he was doing a first-class job, blocking each warren as he went.

Then the bomb went off. I was called to the office and my employer puffed and snorted telling me that I had given permission to the biggest poacher in the county and I must want my head examined. 'I never know where the damn fellow is.' 'That's just it, Sir; it used to be like that, but now I know exactly where he is.' In the end I was told just to 'watch the damn man'. In time the farm manager and the boss came to look at Bunny's work, and they found it good, too.

By the time the fall came I had Bunny helping me on the field and with a bit of outside feeding. He even began to wash and shave, and with a promise of

coming beating he was like a dog with two tails. However, after a time I grew worried that the bags were becoming smaller, particularly one day after some of the best drives; I was now sure that some birds went missing each week. Bunny! Not Bunny – but it had to be. 'You've let me down, Bunny. Why, you ...' He assured me he would not even think of it.

The following Saturday, Bunny's eyes were on overtime. The last but one drive he came to me, he had seen who it was, there were three of them – all the birds from eight and nine stands dumped in the ditch to pick up on the way home. I sorted out the birds for the Guns, hung the rest and paid the beaters, all of whom left except three who had trouble with their van – it was often broke down – but they would fix it and close the gate. That was the end of them!

Bunny was sent for at the office and given a few bob. Also, and more important, he became rabbit catcher on 2,000 acres and was paid for it, plus he kept one of his beady eyes on the estate. He said to me one day, 'It was good luck for me when you caught me poaching'. 'No, it wasn't luck,' I told him. 'I think like a poacher, my old father taught me and taught me well. He was a poacher, but he became a damn sight better keeper to the end of his days.'

(Jim's grandfather was head keeper and his father a keeper for Sir Theodore Brinkman at Winkfield Place, Windsor, Berkshire from 1900 to 1920.)

A POINT OF VIEW

There *are* still those who poach for the sport and not for the reward they may get. However, such poachers are now few and far between in these mercenary days, and most of those who take the risks are only out to make money by selling the ill-gotten booty from their gang raids.

The old-fashioned type of poacher loved the out-of-doors with all the creatures of the fields and woods. The call of the wild was in his blood and he went poaching because he could not resist it. Mainly he was a one-for-the-pot man who sought diversion and excitement and enjoyed nature in her many moods. If this had to be his defence, it would be one which gamekeepers would instinctively understand.

It is not possible to live close to nature all one's life and not acquire a fund of wisdom. The poacher may have a full share of faults as do all men, but he has been bred in a tradition which is second nature to him. Steeped in spiritual wildness, there will always be freebooters in our countryside. The poacher is part of our unkempt hedgerows, and may he remain for ever in our heritage.

THE OFFICIAL VIEW

'Sir Ralph Payne Gallwey, great shooting man and writer, wildfowler par excellence and game preserver of the old school, did not sympathise with the 'Robin Hood' popular view of the poacher, nor with the lenient sentences they often received in the courts.

A poacher is, with scarcely an exception, a cowardly, drunken ruffian. He and his wife and children are clothed in rags. His idleness and loafing habits are habitual to him, for he will not accept any honest, well-paid work. If he is not poaching due to the close season, he is committing petty thefts, stealing ducks and chickens or scouring the country to pick up information for future nocturnal larceny of game.

He cannot run, he is too heavy and bloated from drink to do so, but he can sneak about in fine style under the shelter of walls and ditches or among shadows. He is, however, a fine fighter, always provided there are five or six poachers to one or two keepers for he has not the courage to fight unless the odds are greatly on his side.

Among a dozen bad characters the poacher can be detected almost to a certainty. Why? Because he is sure to have the worst looking countenance of the lot. His restless, suspicious leer, hollow eyes, alehouse face and his stooping, shambling gait proclaim him at once – not to mention his clothes. Even they tell his trade, the knee-worn trousers, bloodstained and wide pocketed coat with often bits of spare snaring wire coiled round the buttons, the latter an evidence of poaching that may be frequently found if looked for.

KING OF THE
NORFOLK POACHERS

The biography I Walked by Night written by Lilias Rider Haggard uses the words and the curious spelling of an old Norfolk poacher to tell of an eventful life recalled in lonely old age.

Lilias Rider Haggard was the daughter of the creator of Allan Quartermain, the great African hunter, hero of King Solomon's Mines. Her imagination was fired by the ancient poacher, now in his old age, who had lived a lawless life in the woods and fields of old Norfolk. Wisely she used his words and guesssed at his spelling to give us an authentic record.

Sent to Norwich prison when twelve years old, convicted of taking a rabbit with the evidence against him suitably embroidered, loathed by keeper and landowner alike, the 'King' was able still to carry on his calling, suffering uncomplainingly some fearful beatings but not incapable of dealing out the same medicine.

His tale is a charming, moving and sometimes amusing record of hard and bygone times.

The Seed is Sown

I stayed at school till I was thirteen years of age, but duren that time wen I was a boy about nine year old some thing hapened. I was with father in the garden, it was winter time, and snow on the ground. Well without a thought he shewed me were a hare had been eaten his plants off. I made up my mind wen I saw that that I would get her.

There was a big trap hangen up in the shed, it had hung there as long as I remembered. I got it down wen father was gone, and sit the trap in the snow. Wen I come home from school the next morning of cors the first place I went to was to look at the trap, and you bet I was something pleased to find the hare there. I verry sone beat the life out of her and carried it to Mother. She near had a fit at what I had done, and carried it upstairs and put it under the bed.

As soon as father came home I went to tell him, I had not got far with my tale before he caught me by the coller and gave me the soundest floggen a boy ever received. He thought to stop me from playen those tricks in futur, but it seem that the seed was sowen by that hare, and it did not take long to germate.

Not long after I rember well me and another Boy was goen up a hedge and we found some snars. Of cors I had to make shure how they were put and then we took them up, and not many days after that I tried my hand at that game. I rember well the next morning taken two hares.

'STITCHED UP'

In the village there was large amount of comon land, of corse it was enclosed as there were plenty of rabbitts there and I sone got to work snaren them. Some kind frend gave me away and wen I went one morning there was a Police man and a Keeper there waiten for me. They did give me a chance of getten away with [getting rid of] the rabbitts in my hands, but they swore I had some in a bag. As a matter of fact I never saw any in the bag till they shewed me some.

Well of corse they sumoned me and to make the case as bad as they could they told a lot of lies as well. Wen it came to it the Justice of the Piece sentenced me to a Months hard Labour wich I did at Norwich Castle.

In those days if a lad did a bit rong it was Prison for him, now he is given a chance as a first ofender. Dear Reader, it was hard lines to send a Boy to Prison for killing a rabbitt. No doubt the Maderstrates thought to cure me with a lesson, especially as the Police had painted me so black to them. Be that as it may, I know they soured me to the Laws of the Land by that treatment, though there is no telling if any man would go a diffrent way to what he has in the end. I always was a belever in Fate.

KEEPER BESTED

There was a verry clever keeper come to the next village about this time, and he used to boast that he had forty hen pheasants under wire. He knew all about my Job, and he used to tell People he would get me befor the year was out. Of corse I sone got to know that he had the birds there. He used to talk a lot and tell People that no one could get at them as he had a dog tied up and an alarm gun set.

It was not long before I had hatched a plan. I got a chap to go to him and ask if he had any ferrits to sell and told him to keep his eyes open and look round to se were the gun was fixed. He did and brought me back word of the exact tree the gun was screwed to.

Well first of all I set to work to find a market as I had made up my mind to get them birds and sone I found one about four miles away. The next thing to do was to get a bitch in use wich I did and took with me and let her run wich is an old trick and verry useful wen you have a dog to deal with. I soon found the gun and put that right and then cut a hole in the wire and got evry one of them birds. I did not do that job alone but two of us did – we got safe away to the road and the birds were at there new home befor they were missed.

Of course the rout was out and a lot of enquiries were made and they came and serched my Place but as there were neither Birds nor Feathers they were lost to know what to do. I got just five pounds for them Birds that trip.

A Bag of Rabbitts

There were a Clever Chap and he got thorns and all the Busshes he could colect, and made Burrers for Rabbitts on a medaw. Then he boght a lot of tame rabbits and got some wild ones to run with them – in fact they Bread verry fast. Well he was goen to have all the Publicans and Shop keepers down on Boxing day to turn the place over and he stood to make a bit out of it. He watched this place and the Rabbits verry carefully, but a day or so befor Christmas we got bussy and went and put the nets round that field and scooped the lot. Of corse they all come as arranged and turned the Place over but the game was gone, and that chap had a good bit to say.

I got the creddit for it as I did for evry other Job at that time, wether I was in on it or not but as the Rabbitts were at Lynn, that fell through.

A Bad Beating

I was in a wood one night and had had a few shots wen I walked into four Keepers. Of corse I knew I was beat that time. I had not a chance, and was willing to give in but they knocked me about with sticks and kicked me most onmercifull. Then they got a cart from the farm nearby and took me to the lock up and left me.

The next morning I was nearly Dead, so bad that the Police had to send for the Doctor and wen he had looked at me he ordered me to be taken to Lynn Ospitall.

I had a verry bad cut head and Brused Boddy. I stayed there for a fortnight and wen I was able to get about and got my Discharge, a Policeman was waiting for me. Well wen it came to it the Keepers swore that I had put up a terrible fight – thretned to shoot them and all that. The Judge did not beleve them, but as I was Poaching I had to get it, but he let me off with twenty one days and told the keepers that they had behaved verry cruele to me. I was sent back to Norwich – to the new Prison on Mousehold this time but they gave me no task there as I was still verry sore. I think the judge had some thing to do with that.

Well the Head Keeper got the sack ... he should not have allowed the other ones to have knocked me about as they did, I supose they thought they were getten some of there own back on me for all the tricks I had played them, but that never stopped me.

REVENGE

The 'King' is returning with his friends from a live pigeon shooting match where he had won the double breech loading section. On the way cycling home, they spotted a pheasant roosting in a tree.

No sooner seen than it was dead, and that started us off. I suppose we all had a merry time and were verry well pleased with ourselves, anyways we soon got bussy in the wood.

That was all right but things bein what they were we were not as careful as we should have been and I expect we made a bit of a racket. Two keepers must have heard us and they come along and was on us befor we knew. One of my mates sone laid one of them out and I had the pleasure of stoppin the other one. He hapened to be the man as had treated me so bad befor, and as by that time we was well in, I did not stop to think or lose the chance of payen some of the score back that I owed.

Well the Game was up for me then, and I knew I must get away as quick as I could or they would be on to me as I was thinking we had hurt both them keepers verry badly and were in for a lot of trubble soon as they was found. So I got to the nearest town and into the train for the North of England before many hours were past.

LAMB STEW

I had lerned how to make my owen nets, and I sone had plenty of them and a pair of lurchers and I knew well how to use both. I rember one night I was out and set a net at a gate and sent my dogs to hunt the field. It turned out that there was lots of lambs in it which I did not know, and the dogs scattered them in all directions. One, I am sorry to say ran at the gate and Broke its neck, which was unfortunate – but me being done, me and my chum was rather pussled to know what to do with it so he suggested we should take it to his house which we did. We sckined it and Burried the skin the same night a mile from home. Strange to say that lamb was never missed, at least if it was we never herd of it.

A Haul of Partridge

The rearin season soon came round again and I got to know that they had reared a large number of tame partridges not far from my place. There was a chance for me, and with a little spyen and some enquirs, I sone made out were they were feeden. The night before they came into season, my mate and me took the net and dragged a large medaw and caught one hundred and sixty, I believe it was. Of corse they were missed and they came to me stright away, but the birds were in Norwich by that time, so I had the laugh of them again.

Hiding

I have hid and seen the Keepers go past me many a time. On one ocation I was in a wood at Whaton and three keepers were looking for me. I had killed a bird within a few yards of them. While they were looking for me I got out of the wood and shot all the way home. Of corse it is a useless job looking for one man in a wood wen it is dark, he have only to lay down or stand still and let those that are looken pass him.

In a genrall way the keepers are a lot more excited than the Poacher. I have often smiled to myself wen I have got away to think what a stew they were in, wen they found me gone. If I have had a gun I have often fired it to let them know that I was gone – and wich way. It is a rum job for the Keepers to catch a lone Poacher wen it is dark.

One time I rember I was surrounded by keepers, I could hear them talking while I was layen there quite still and as sone as I could I drew away from them and they never heard me or knew I was there.

NIGHT SIGHT

Years ago we used to use a sight of this kind. Cut a pair of ears out of a stuff piece of leather and use it on the muzzle of a gun – so it look like rabbitts ears on the end. Wen the Poacher could see the bird between the ears he was shure of his kill but since then the Eleumintaed sight is much more used and the four point ten gun. I have tried it with a lot of success. The gun in the old days was a muzle loader with the Barrells cut off to eighteen inches and as small a bore as we could get, mostly sixteen bore.

A FISHY TALE

There was a big hall with a sort of ornamental fish Pond beside it, with some very fine trout in it. The water was quite shallow not more than a foot deep. Those fish were talked about quite a lot so the two of us went there one moonlight night and captured the lot of them. We had a good haul and there was one, a fine fish of the Rainbow class, weighed Just over nine pound.

We got the fish to Lynn befor they were missed but a few days after I saw in the paper that a gentleman had caught a fine trout wich he was haven stuffed – I knew the fisherman verry well.

I went and asked the dealer who he had sold the fish we cought to, and it was the same Gentleman that had caught the fish – so much for his Catchen it.

THE NORFOLK HINGLE

A snare is used were the Phesants creep through the hedges, a bow stick being put round the hingle to make the bird drop his head. Another way is to make a hole in the ground three inch deep and two inch across the top. The hingle is laid round the hole that have already been partly filled with white peas. He come along and put his head in the hole, bring the hingle up on his neck and is verry sone dead. The hingle is also used in the hare and rabbitt runs in the long grass in a wood with a bender over the hingle to keep his head down to the level of the snare.

The hingle for phesants is made of four strands of plible copper wire, as sone as he pull the wire tight he is dead.

DOGS

I had one old dog so perfectly trained if he walked to a field gate he knew well enough if there was a hare on that field. He would just whine and stand still till the net was ready and the hare would be quickly dead. Me and that dog killed hundreds of hares and rabbits. I kept him till like me he could not work any longer. If there was a keeper or Policeman about he knew and would let me know as plain as if he could speak.

I had another small retrever bitch I trained for the gun at night. She could find a phesant up a tree as well as I could all I had to do was to watch her and she would find them. As sone as the bird was killed I had it in my hand but like a lot of useful things she died before she was very old. I well rember going to a wood not far from Bungay. I shot a bird from a tree and the bitch brought it to me growling. There were two keepers within twenty yards of me, but I simply crawled in the wood and laid down and they passed me by.

EPITAPH FOR A POACHER

My memry often goes back to them days wen I played the game all out and made a good thing out of it for many years. Well. I think to myself, I have had my share of pleasure and my share of trubbles and now I am alone and my work nearly done, and I make myself content until the finish. I have rote these lines and told what I know not to lern the young man of today the art of taken game but Just to show how one man can dupe a lot of others. I am now seventy five, and if I had my time to come over again I would still be what I have been – A Poacher.

BLOODY AFFRAY

The history of poaching is peppered with accounts of fights and dirty deeds. Sometimes the keeper, young and scared maybe, was responsible by over-reacting; at others the paochers had come with the full intention of using violence if confronted. Keeper Wilkins had his share of battles, once being all but killed, but his approach of firmness and fairness and treating the captured poacher kindly seemed to pay off, and he suffered less violence than many.

However, good men died on both sides, beaten, maimed in man traps, lacerated by spring guns, bludgeoned or shot. Such deaths and injuries were futile, all laid at the door of silly pheasants and lolloping hares, but man is born to trouble as the sparks fly upwards and it was surely inevitable that those as opposed as keeper and poacher would come to blows sometimes.

POACHER'S REVENGE

It was not unknown for wires to be set deliberately in fairly conspicuous places where the sharp-eyed keeper would be likely to find them. This was best done in the dead of winter with the weather at its coldest. In the event of the keeper failing to see the wires, a third party might give him a friendly warning as to their presence.

The keeper would set up a careful ambush and then sit up for a night or more waiting to nab a poacher; but he, of course, was either snug in bed or up to his tricks on another part of the estate, and chuckling to himself at the thought of how cold his enemy was getting and how frustrated he would feel as the cold light of dawn appeared over the oaks and he knew he had failed.

One gang came unstuck trying this dodge and the keeper had the last laugh. The poachers set a row of snares right against the keeper's garden hedge and sent an informer to tell him where they were. The keeper was an old hand and sent back the message that he was too cunning to be caught out by such an old trick, and that they were wasting their time.

Disgruntled, the informer returned to his mates and told them the sad news, so they returned to the hedge to take up the wires which would no longer serve a useful purpose. To their surprise the keeper, backed by two hefty assistants, leaped out at them and bagged them all. Their little subterfuge resulted in fifty shillings or three weeks inside.

Sometimes the poachers would fire off a volley of shots in one part of the estate, thus luring the keeper and his men to the spot where they would keep watch. In the meantime the poachers would be hard at their work on the far side of the property.

ALARUMS AND EXCURSIONS

Not infrequently the poacher became violent when cornered. The best advice was for the keeper to go armed with nothing more than a stout cudgel. For him to boast openly of knuckledusters, cosh or revolver and the like would do no more than ensure that his enemies went out similarly or even better armed. The run-of-the-mill poacher knew this too; on one occasion a gang persuaded a road-mender to join them on an expedition as they were short of numbers. However, he showed every intention of taking his heavy hammer with him, a formidable weapon. It was the poachers themselves who, with some difficulty, dissuaded him.

The keeper found himself in a 'You win, I lose' situation when the going got rough. Were he bested by the poachers the locals would smile behind their hands and say 'serve him right', for many folk then – as now – had the idea that a poacher was a romantic Robin Hood striking a blow for the freedom of the oppressed. In the event of the keeper prevailing, all the sympathy went to his victim and no-one took any notice of the keeper, who could but claim that he was dong no more than the job for which he was being paid.

A captured poacher was entitled to fair treatment once he had surrendered, and a good keeper would earn grudging respect by humane behaviour. Strong-arm tactics would not be resorted to unless the poacher showed signs of fight, but when this did occur the keeper made sure he got in his blow first and saw to it that it was a good one.

The worst fears of the keeper were of encountering night poachers armed with guns for shooting pheasants from trees. Such men would think nothing of murder, shooting down a policeman or keeper as easily as they would a dog. 'It is so easily done; merely a slight pressure on the trigger and the antagonist is dead.' These men would be shown no fair play whatsoever, but attacked and disarmed before they knew what was happening.

A bold keeper was advised to hide behind a tree trunk and spring out at the leader with the gun as he passed, and make every effort to grapple for the trigger and fire it into the air before it could do more serious damage. The sudden surprise of such an attack and a quick and efficient disarming took the steam out of the poachers almost before they could think of putting up violent resistance – but such an encounter called for enormous courage, just as much as it does today.

THE THIGH CRACKER

Made by local blacksmiths, these man traps rejoiced under a number of trade names such as 'the crusher', 'the body squeezer' and 'the thigh cracker'. They were monsters, and came in a variety of designs, some with sharks' teeth, others with regular rows of long spikes, and some with a series of rounded blades which promised almost instant amputation. Richard Jefferies called the man trap 'the iron wolf'. Old relics still survive in museums in sufficient numbers to suggest they were a widely used deterrent. Some, such as the 'boy traps', caught merely at the ankles; others caught at the waist – one of the latter was eight feet long and weighed in at more than a hundredweight. There can be no doubt that in those days of primitive medicine and no National Health, one encounter with a man trap would certainly have led to amputation, probably to gangrene and thus, inevitably, to death.

An eye-witness report from Hampshire at the end of the eighteenth century read as follows: 'The hardened banditii, disregarding the notice of what was prepared for their destruction, ventured into the night, as had been their custom, where no less than four of them were found in the morning caught in these terrible engines. Three had their thighs broke by the crackers and traps and the fourth was found dead in a body squeezer ... I saw the poor wretches after they had been taken from these destructive engines.'

Advertisements for man traps appeared alongside those for cast-iron stoves and kitchen utensils in the brochures of Black Country iron works. The latest in high technology for the more kindly landowner was the 'humane man trap', so-called because it merely held the poacher captive without inflicting the fearful injuries of the spiked versions. However, there were doubts as to whether such 'humanitarian' claims could be supported: one eloquent in the argument against them would certainly have been the Rev Mr Lawson who was strolling and botanising one day in a plantation near Barking Hill.

Inadvertently he stepped on a 'humane' man trap and ... 'although some people were attracted to the spot by his cries, they were unable to release him; and he remained for nearly an hour and half suffering the most excruciating pain before the gamekeeper could be found to unlock this cruel instrument, and extricate the worthy gentleman, whose leg was found to be much lacerated.'

Scrambled Eggs

Here John Wilkins the nineteenth-century Hertfordshire gamekeeper,
deals with an egg thief.

When I thought the poachers had laughed enough at my expense I stepped up to Harry who was still on the grin and said, 'Yes and so you are fond of bird's eggs, aren't you?'

In a moment his countenance changed and the grin grew ghastly as he angrily asked what I meant. 'I mean' said I 'that pocket full of pheasant's eggs you took from that clump of briars yonder.'

And before he knew what I was up to, I struck his pockets with the flat of my hand and smash went the rotten eggs I had planted in the nest for him. At this he began cursing and swearing, but I merely remarked, 'Good Morning, Harry'. Turning to the other two I observed, 'You won't be so fast to laugh at John Wilkins another time, perhaps.'

From Wild Sports of the Highlands *by Charles St John.*

THE BITER BIT

The keepers themselves in the Highlands as long as the poachers do not interfere too much with their masters' sport are rather anxious to avoid a collision with these 'Hieland Lads'. For although they never ill-use keepers, in the savage manner that English poachers so frequently do, I have known of keepers too smart 'gentlemen' to carry their master's game, taken prisoner by poachers on the hill and obliged to accompany them over their master's ground and carry the game killed on it all day. They have then either been sent home or, if troublesome, the poachers have tied them hand and foot and left them at some marked spot of the muir, sending a boy or a shepherd to release them some hours afterwards.

RONALD, THE HIGHLAND POACHER

A finer specimen than Ronald I never saw. As he passes through the streets of a country town the men give him plenty of walking room while not a girl in the street but stops to look after him ... He is about 26 years old his height more than six feet with limbs somewhat between those of Hercules and Apollo, he steps along the street with the good natured, self-satisfied swagger of a man who knows all the women are admiring him.

He is dressed in a plain, grey kilt and jacket with an otterskin purse and a low skull cap with a long peak from below which his quick eye seems to take in at a glance everything which is passing round him. A man whose life is spent much in hunting and the pursuit of wild animals acquires unconsciously a peculiar restless and quick expression of eye, appearing always to be in search of something. As he walked into my room followed by his two magnificent dogs he would have made a subject worthy of Landseer in his best moments.

RONALD IS ATTACKED BY KEEPERS

Ronald was awoken from his sleep in the wooden recess of the shealing by five men coming in saying that they had tracked him there, that he was caught at last and must come along with them. Two of them went to the bed to pull him out.

So I just pit them under me and kept them both down with one knee. A third chiel then came up with a bit painted wand and told me that he was a constable and I said to him, 'John Cameron, my man, you'd be better employed making shoes at home than coming here to disturb a quiet lad like me.'

At last the laird's keeper who I knew well enough although he didn't know me whispered to the rest and all three made a rush at me while the chiels below me tried to get up too. The keeper was the only one with any pluck among them and he sprang on my neck and as he was a clever-like lad I began to get sore pressed. Just then, however, I lifted up my left hand and pulled one of the sticks that served as rafters out of the roof above me, and my blood was getting quite mad like and the Lord only knows what would have happened if they hadn't all been a bit frightened seeing me with the stick, when a part of the roof came falling on them so they left me and went to the other end of the shealing.

One of the lads below my knee got hurt in this scuffle too, indeed, one of his ribs was broken so I helped to lift him up and put him on the bed. The others threatened me a good deal but didna like the look of the bit constable's staff I had in my hand. At last they begged me in the Lord's name to leave the shealing and go my way in peace. I went at them with my staff but they didna bide my coming and were all tumbling out of the door in a heap before I was near them. I could'na help laughing to see them.

(Ronald allowed the keepers to sleep in one end of the shealing for it was a foul night; his boy watched them for half the night and he for the rest of it. In the morning he gave them all breakfast and left, but all was not over yet.)

ROUND TWO

I had my gun and four brace of grouse which they looked at very hard indeed but I did not let them lay hands on anything. When I had got a few hundred yards away I missed my shot belt so I went back and found that the keeper had it and would not give it up. I took him by the coat and shook him a bit and he soon gave it me but he could'na keep his hands off and as I turned away he struck me a sair blow with a stick on my back.

So I turned to him and 'deed I was near beating him weel but after all I thocht that the poor lad was only doing his duty, so I give him a lift into the burn taking care not to hurt him but he got a grand ducking and Lord – how he did swear! I was thinking it was lucky the twa dogs were not with me for there would have been wild work in that shealing. Bran cannot bide a scuffle but he must join in and the other dog would go and help him and Lord help the man they took hold of – he would be in a bad way before I could get this one off his throat.

HIS FIRST POACHER

One morning when I was on the watch I heard a 'scrunch, scrunch' on the frozen beech leaves and took up my gun ready for a shot as I thought it was some kind of vermin on the prowl. Presently I saw a man step into the path, look round the bend and then go back to the edge of the wood. Here he knelt down and began feeling about in the ferns. It was about half past two in the morning and I could see only the outline of the man as he groped on his knees.

I thought he was after pheasant eggs and I made ready to catch him. Taking off my coat and jacket thus exposing my blue shirt sleeves, I crept up to within a few yards of my man and, with a sudden spring, landed on his back catching hold of his collar. He was a big, strong man and I thought I was in for a tough job but I never saw such a total collapse in my life. The moment he felt my weight on his back and looked up at me he seemed to come over all limp.

This man turned out to be a good plucked 'un and a rough fighting man who would stand up for a good bout any day. Had I not been so quick and frightened and unnerved him, he could have flung me in the gorse with the greatest of ease and made his escape, but fortune favours the brave and, maybe the rash.

THE END OF DABBER

Wilkins finds a long-dead hare which he saves for his ferrets but on second thoughts stitches up its wounds – for it had been badly damaged by crows and was already beginning to smell somewhat. He finds another use for it, and returns to where he had seen 'Dabber' checking some empty snares the day before.

I tucked her head in the noose of the snare and drew it tight; then I took the slack of the wire and see-sawed it against the stems to rub the bark off, pulled out the fluck [fur] to show where she had torn herself in dashing about.

I waited and watched and at about seven in the morning arrived Dabber with his gun and beats the plantation down to where his snares were set. When he got to within fifteen or twenty yards he saw old Sarah [country name for a hare] and dropping his gun he rushed forward and fell flat on top of her. He took her out of the snare and pocketed her while still lying flat on the ground. Then he got up and carefully removed every scrap of fluck after which he went back a little way into the wood, kicking up the moss and earth and buried the fluck underneath it stamping it down with his feet.

Next he took some earth and rubbed over the white thorn bush in the place where the snare had barked it, then brought some leaves and strewed over the place where Sarah had scratched up the earth under the snare. After this he made everything look as if it had not been disturbed, then standing a little way back he took a good view and coming back, placed a twig here and there and smeared a little dirt over a spot in the bark that showed white. At last he seemed quite satisfied and indeed, one might have passed the place without ever noticing that anything had recently been caught there.

Off he goes with one-eyed Sarah and after going about twenty yards or so, he thought he'd take a peep at her. Just as he was doing this, I stepped up behind him on tiptoe saying, 'How is it? A good one Dabber?'

WILKINS LOSES HIS GUN

I saw a man creep through the hedge and proceed to examine the snares. When he discovered the leveret he glanced cautiously all around, then removed it from the wire still alive and put it in his pocket. The animal gave a kick and jumped out of one side of his smock frock but, being half dead, it travelled slowly so he fell on his hands and knees and crawled after it. Before he could reach it I sprang forward and caught him by the collar, the leveret escaping.

We had a sharp tussle for some time; he managed to get up off the ground and as I held him with my left hand only, he got hold of my gun which I held in my right. Seizing the stock with one hand and the barrel with the other, he gave a twist and wrenched it away from me. Letting go his collar I immediately seized the gun and we struggled together to obtain possession of it, sometimes he got it away from me for a few seconds, and then I would recapture it again and had it to myself for a little while, then we both had hold of it and so the fight went on, until at last I got it fairly away from him, when he ran at me to knock me down. I struck out at him aiming at his head, but he put up his hand to ward off the blow.

Then clenching both hands round the weapon he backed me against a stub which had the effect of nearly upsetting me. Seeing me totter he made a rush at me to pin me down so I clubbed my weapon and struck at him with the butt end. He dodged the blow and caught hold of the butt, so that I was left half on the ground clutching the barrels and as these were wet and slippery he soon got the gun away from me.

We had now been at it for about ten minutes and were both pretty well blown, still I had plenty of fight left in me. I sprang to my feet and seeing that he was feeling for a knife kept on twisting him round so that he could not get at it. I had nothing to defend myself with or to attack him now and as fast as I approached him he kept prodding me with the gun barrel and kicking at me. Cocking the gun he shouted to me to stand off or he'd be the death of me but luckily in the struggle both caps has fallen off the nipples so I escaped unhurt.

Finding this he clubbed the gun and threatened to smash my brains out. He was much bigger and stronger than I and weighed over fourteen stone whilst I only weighed eight or nine stone. I told him I knew his name and so reluctantly he departed, going right into the wood.

(*Returning later with reinforcements, Wilkins found Alexander gone from the scene but discovered his gun lying within a few yards of the wood edge. After some months Alexander was arrested and tried for attempted murder. Thanks largely to Wilkins' evidence – he re-enacted the fight in the witness box – he was convicted to two years in Devizes Prison. When released he turned over a new leaf and became an honest man; he was of respectable stock, his father being a Methodist Minister.*)

A Bloody Business

Wilkins and two companions surprise a large gang of poachers netting hares. He shoots two of their dogs and is making arrests when his less experienced companions aggravate things and the poachers show fight.

The two poachers kept me on the ground with their knobbed sticks, thump thump like two blacksmiths at the anvil. I tried to rise and was knocked down again but at last managed to stagger to my feet holding my gun and with this I struck a smart blow at one of the men. He bobbed his head to save himself and the gun struck him on the thumb nail cutting it nearly off. This did not however, stop the blow for the gun barrel struck the ground at our feet, breaking off short at the stock and causing me to fall forward on my hands and knees. Then it was thump thump on my head again, more anvil business. I had a tough job to get on my feet again, but I managed to at last having the butt of the gun left to defend myself with.

Now ensued a sharper fight than before. I warded off a good many blows, not only with the butt end of the gun but also my left arm so that after a time the latter got numbed and I knew one of the bones was broken which turned out afterwards to be the case. I used the stump of the gun to ward off five blows out of six. They told my master afterwards that I received enough blows to my head to kill a horse; they said that the blows sounded like a man threshing on a barn floor.

(*His assailants left to chase off the two other keepers who had offered no help to Wilkins in his hour of need.*)

... The men came back to where I lay groaning in the ditch and I distinctly heard one of them say: 'Here's the chap in the ditch; kill the devil, drag him out and settle him.' 'Where is he?' said another; 'I don't see him. I know he's there for I heard him groan; that's where he is; bring him out and settle him.' Then I held my breath as they poked their gate net sticks into the ditch and I felt one scrape over my legs and punch into my calves. 'I felt him; bring him out,' said one and the other forthwith got down into the ditch and began to pull me out. I was too badly battered to care much what they did with me now and I was perfectly resigned to my fate.

(*One of the poachers persuades the others not to kill Wilkins and taking guns, dead dogs and the nets they leave the scene and Wilkins more dead than alive.*)

71

… I rested for fifteen or twenty minutes and then made an effort to rise and get out of the ditch. I first got upon my hands and knees and remained there for about five minutes, then I made a move to crawl out but only fell back again. I had another long rest until after repeated attempts I managed to get out. I was weak from loss of blood and giddy from blows in the head and my left arm was broken. After several tumbles and long rests I staggered like a drunken man into Church Road about two hundred yards from Stanstead. I met the seven or eight men who had been sent to fetch my dead body from Ryecroft ditch.

After laying for a fortnight I was well enough to go down to Saffron Walden and give evidence before the magistrate. All six men were sent for trial at Chelmsford.

THE GANTON AFFAIR

There were times when a confrontation between poachers and keepers could not be avoided, when the constant battle of wits exploded in simple violence, dark deeds and tragedy in the shadowy woodlands. On the night of 25 November 1904, six gamekeepers from the neighbouring estates of Sherburn and Ganton in North Yorkshire confronted three poachers, with tragic results. The keepers had spent the day pheasant shooting on the Wolds, and it had been arranged that they should meet to go duck shooting at nine o'clock. They knew that poachers could well be active that night but guessed that their presence shooting would act as a deterrent.

According to Mr Thomas Gambling, head keeper to Mr Pickering, the three poachers were seen standing in a row at a distance of about thirty yards. One of them, Dobson, shouted 'Stand back, or I shall shoot'. As the keepers continued to advance, apparently Dobson fired and hit Thomas Gambling in the face and front of his waistcoat; a second shot injured him in the thigh and groin. The keeper's acccount maintained that almost immediately a second poacher fired, fatally wounding another keeper, Thomas Atkinson. As the other keepers closed with the poachers, Dobson hit Gambling over the head with the butt of his gun, before he was finally overpowered.

On the keepers' part, one shot was fired at the poachers the moment Atkinson fell, and one of them was heard to cry out 'He has shot me!' as they scrambled over the fence and made off in the direction of the main road. Later, claims were made in court that the poachers fired three times and the keepers twice. All the poachers' guns were muzzle-loaders and all the stocks were broken off in the ensuing struggle.

After the fight the keeper Gambling was found lying in a pool of blood. He was lifted onto a hurdle and carried to the hotel in Sherburn. Keeper Card was dizzy and bleeding and was given a tot of brandy by the station master at Weaverthorpe station. Atkinson was found to be dead and was taken home on a cart. The three poachers were arrested and brought to Scarborough Police Station where they were charged: they were William 'Curly Bill' Hovington, his son Charles and the third man Dobson.

The poachers' tale differed from that of keepers on all the main points. At his trial Charles Hovington claimed that on the afternoon in question he had gone to the top of Oliver's Mount and there met his father and Dobson; from where they had left for Sherburn to shoot pheasants. On meeting the six keepers, they had set off as fast as they could run, but were set upon by the keepers' dogs. He said that one of the keepers had fired and brought him down; Hovington had then put his gun to his shoulder but it did not fire; he fired the other barrel and a dog ran off yelping.

His father, William, said that after his son was shot he had gone on for another twenty yards or so before crying out that he could go no further. William added that a further shot had hit him in the leg and he had fallen to the ground; as he did so his gun went off. When asked by the judge if he had seen a man fall he said he had not. The three said that then they had begun to fight with the keepers.

The judge decided on the evidence before him that the keepers had not fired the first shot and that all three poachers were determined to fight to the death if needs be, and with one keeper killed and a second badly wounded, this is what they had done. Not only had they fired their guns with intent to murder, but had used the butts of the weapons as clubs. He concluded that it was not for poaching that the three had gone out, but simply to do battle with 'the authorities', in this case in the form of the keepers. It sounds a story depressingly familiar today.

William Hovington and Thomas Dobson were both sentenced to ten years in prison, and Charles Hovington, on slightly lesser charges, got seven years. As he left the dock Charles saluted and said 'Thank you, Sir'. One might reflect that under the circumstances they had got off lightly.

A CLOSE SHAVE

From James Knight

This poacher was different, a gun man, and well known round about when I got a new job in Oxfordshire. Not only did he keep the keepers on their toes with the bang of his gun, but the employers heard it too, so there was some friction and harsh words between keepers and bosses most mornings, my employer and me included – and still the bangs went on.

I chose a clump of nettles to squat behind this evening – no reason, just me and my dog at peace. Another drag on my tobacco and all at peace with the world when – bang! My labrador, Bruce, set off as usual and by the time I was in pursuit, he had snatched the rabbit from beneath the poacher's outstretched hand. The poacher had only one way out, straight to the blackthorn hedge interlaced with blackberry and dog rose: a formidable wall. I was closing fast and could see him trying to find a weak spot to get through.

At that moment and about seventy yards away, my gun 'accidentally' went off. He went through that hedge as though he had a rocket in his trousers; I got the rabbit and his gun he dropped, but not him. Sod it! So near and yet so far. But ...

there was something I did not know. The poacher finished up at the surgery, and the doctor, duty bound, reported it to the Law.

Our local man arrived with two well-dressed CID men, not very nice men either of them. After the Gestapo had satisfied themselves that I did not 'have gun, will travel', they told me I might be summonsed for discharging a gun to maim or injure, which I duly was; and soon found myself on the way to court. At 10am I walked into that great place, and for once in my life I was afraid.

I had already rehearsed my answers. A mean-looking man wagged a finger at me and said, 'You shot this man to inflict injury, didn't you?' 'No, sir.' 'Then you just tell the court how this man's injuries occurred if you did not shoot him.' Out of my depth in such a place I forgot my rehearsals, and this is what I said:

'While chasing this poacher and shouting "Stop!", I caught my foot in a bramble and (wait for it) arse over head I went and off went the gun.' There was much laughter somewhere above, I looked round and up there was a balcony full of people. 'Order in Court!' I was cleared on all counts.

Two weeks later the police demanded my gun be inspected by an Oxford gun-smith to see if it would go off if dropped. According to his report, everything was so badly worn it was even dangerous as a wall piece, not to mention the hole half way up the right-hand barrel. I was told by His Worship to scrap it before it shot me. He was almost right, and to this day I carry the scars when 'Old Bessie' blew up – not very funny.

At least there were no more bangs, and I had many a pat on the back from my neighbours and I never did see that chap again.

ROTTERS

I found blood, trails of it, and deer hair and guts inside a hazel wood off a deer track. I knew a woman and two kids gathering firewood were part of it, but how? I saw them turn up one day, so I made for a point in the wood near where the guts were, and I hid.

Within an hour I heard something 'slap' and a deer went past, blood pouring from its ribs. She went twenty yards and dropped, still alive. Two gypsies, heads bent, came chasing down the deer track. I dropped the first one, the other stumbled on his mate, and I finished him off with a piledriver in the back.

The woman and two kids at the top end snapping and gathering wood, plus the odd cough or two, sent the deer walking down the track beneath the hazels. Two yards to the side of the track squatted the gypsies armed with very large catapults, and as the deer passed, its rib cage was but a yard or two from their outstretched arms.

The razor-sharp missiles cut straight into its lungs; they were triangular mower-knife blades from an old grass cutter, sharpened on all three sides. I tried these weapons on sacks of wheat and ten gallon drums: terrible damage at six yards. These men were not poachers; they were bastards, murderers, and they couldn't fight, either. You cannot even think of comparing these wretches with the old village poacher. They are from different worlds.

Spring Guns and 'Engines'

These featured in the late eighteenth and early nineteenth centuries. Early models were crude flintlock pistols fixed to a tree on a pivot with a wire to the trigger. As the poacher's leg caught the wire it directed the gun straight at his legs and further pressure sent ounce lumps of lead flying at him. Some keepers were not particular and aimed the gun higher to cover the poacher's head. Some fired 4in iron bolts.

Many victims were quite innocent, unlearned or unobservant enough not to be able to read the warning notices. One poor woman out gathering mushrooms in Norfolk trod on the trip wire of an 'abominable engine' and no less than fifty-five shots lodged in the upper part of her legs which were cut about terribly. A small boy climbed a bank to cut a hedge stick and was cut down by the full charge of a spring gun. A gentleman sent his gardener to prune a tree; as he placed his ladder in position he too was struck down without warning. The three sons of Admiral Wilson entered the preserve with another boy ... one of their dogs touched a spring gun wire and all four were seriously injured.

The redoubtable Col George Hanger in his work *To All Sportsmen* recommended not only spring guns but a six-pound cannon overlooking the wood. He recommended loading with marbles and clay balls bored with holes and baked in a kiln. These made a fearful whistling when fired and when combined with the marbles would have a devastating effect on anyone unlucky enough to come under fire. Clay rather than iron was used in the charge only in order to spare standing timber from damage: the limb of a tree was a far more valuable resource than the limb of a poacher.

Oddly enough it was the poachers who were safest of all the rural community from these fearful devices, because they were wary and knew what to look for. A poaching gang arrested in Windsor Park in 1813 was armed with long poles in order to set off any spring guns they might encounter. Some resourceful poachers drove cattle ahead of them in the danger zones; others who found spring guns, re-set them in places where the gamekeeper would be hoist with is own petard. In one famous case the son of an estate owner set off to shoot the woods in the absence of the keeper, trod on the fatal wire and was severely wounded in the legs.

Motor Mishap

The keeper stood watching a suspicious van moving very slowly along one of his tracks late in the evening. It was the type of vehicle which any self-respecting village bobby would stop and search on sight. The keeper decided to show himself and gently move in on the intruders, and let them know that the estate was zealously guarded.

He was seen instantly and the van suddenly roared off as the driver hit the throttle. But at that very moment there came a muffled boom from the vehicle which lurched to a stop. A pall of smoke, dust and rust flew from the passenger side and the keeper ran up to investigate. The two men had indeed been on a

poaching expedition and were about to fire at a bird in the roadside field when they saw the keeper in the mirror. The sudden act of snatching the gun back in through the open window and the lurching acceleration of the van, had caused the weapon to go off, blowing a jagged hole in the door. Neither poacher was injured, but both were badly shaken.

EPITAPHS

Two gravestones stand side by side in the Hampshire village of North Baddesley, both marking the demise of Charles Smith. One reads: 'In memory of Charles Smith who suffered at Winchester on 23rd March 1822 for resisting by firearms his apprehension by the gamekeeper of VISCOUNT LORD PALMERSTON, when found in Hough Coppice looking after what is called game. Aged Thirty years.'

The companion stone gives a fuller and less favourable account of the deceased: 'Charles Smith was convicted at Winchester Assizes of 'attempting to murder'. A watcher named Robert Snellgrove approached Smith to identify him. Snellgrove, quite a youth, was alone and unarmed. Smith with a companion and armed, fired at close quarters the whole contents of his gun into Snellgrove's body. In 1822 "attempt to murder" was a capital crime.'

IN THE FAMILY

In 1884 John Lowther was sentenced to death for shooting Thomas Metcalf, head-keeper to the Duke of Zetland at Lofthouse in Cleveland. Metcalf was shot in the right knee and groin, there being no fewer than seventy-eight gunshot wounds and a great amount of shot in the unfortunate man's bones; many of the wounds were lacerated. At the same time as firing at Metcalf, Lowther had wounded a second keeper who was with Metcalf and chasing him.

The coincidence was that forty years before, Lowther's father had murdered a keeper named Moffat in the woods of Mulgrave near Whitby. The father had been tried at York Assizes in 1844 and sentenced to death. Petitions were raised to have the sentence reduced, however, and it was commuted to transportation for life. Lowther was deported to Australia but in attempting to escape, was shot down by the prison guards in the very same part of his body as he had shot Moffat.

HARD LUCK FOR PETER

Angus Nudds is the redoubtable keeper at Tetworth in Bedfordshire. His book The Woods Belong to Me *is a fascinating account of a long and varied gamekeeping life. Angus relates how his first job had been as bird starver. He discovered some pheasants feeding round an old pea stack and found that if he soaked a pea, threaded it on a fish hook, and attached it to a short length of string, he could regularly get himself a bird in those hungry times. He was promoted from this task and a new lad, Peter, was left in his place.*

I was about to leave when I said to the new lad, 'If you want to catch a pheasant, put one of these soaked peas on a fish hook, tie a piece of string to the hook and you will get one.' About ten days later it appeared that one of the keepers was walking along the hedgerow watching his pheasants feeding round the stacks when all of a sudden one of them flew in the air about thirty feet and crashed down again. The keeper ran round to the other side of the field because he had seen the pheasant was flapping nearer and nearer to the hedge on that side. There he saw Peter with about a hundred and fifty yards of fishing line out and a cock pheasant firmly attached to the other end, gradually hauling him in, hand over hand. Unfortunately, Peter was given the sack but I was more lucky than I deserved for I got away scot free to start my gamekeeping career.

A PRICKLY PROBLEM

Gil Gaylor, the Gatcombe Park poacher, writes of his experiences in the 1970s.

Once when out with Brian we were confronted by Eddie the keeper and two of his shooting pals. Eddie was convinced that Brian had a ferret and nets concealed in his outsized pockets; Brian offered no resistance to a search, but Eddie quickly yanked out his hand with a curse. Very carefully Brian then put his own hand to his pocket and slowly drew out a large hedgehog. He placed it at Eddie's feet and we both broke out into laughter while Eddie and his pals fumed.

A few days later Brian met Eddie again, when he *did* have nets and ferrets tucked away. However, Eddie did not search him after the hedgehog episode, for fear of being made a fool of twice!

THE TRICKY ONE

The American duck trappers with their wire mesh cages accounted for hundreds of thousands of illegally taken wildfowl. One warden reckoned that in his lifetime he had taken and destroyed over 15,000 traps. In this tale from Harry M. Walsh's book The Outlaw Gunner, *Jim the warden outwits a lone trapper.*

The warden noticed some bits of old corn cob floating from the creek. To his experienced eye this meant a trapper baiting above and was a highly significant discovery. Jim could sense the gimlet eye of the trapper upon him as he carefully avoided the area. To him a duck trapper was worth a hundred regular cases and he didn't want to frighten his man away. Quickly he decided where the trap had been set and marked it for a return that night. The tide of chance had swung against the trapper.

Jim watched the stars creep slowly across the heavens; cold, bored and cramped, he wished for the comfort of his bed and fought the urge to return home. No-one cared for a duck or a duck sheriff, so why bother?

The abrupt silence which came with the cessation of the ducks' feeding alerted the warden. With their startled flight he felt sure his vigil had been worthwhile. The ducks acted as sentinels for hunted and hunter alike. Reassured by the presence of the duck, the trapper materialised from the night. He was aware that each moment spent at the trap was dangerous for him and he moved like a shadow about his work.

Holding a light between his knees onto the ducks, he began placing them alive in the bags. Each bird was grasped expertly by the bill to prevent fluttering. Live birds could be released with a twist of the drawstring, carrying all the evidence away with them. In the safety of his home, the trapper would kill his ducks with a twist of the wrist. He had an unofficial record of killing two hundred in two minutes flat. A nearby two gallon coffee can was full of duck bands [rings]; they ran nearly to three per cent of all ducks taken.

Warden Jim's enemy had walked into the trap but the trap had yet to be slammed shut. Alone at night on a desolate marsh with a cornered and potentially dangerous man, he had to be careful. Wardens had been lost before.

'We've got you surrounded', spoke the warden softly as he eased to within a few paces of the outlaw. 'Be a shame to have to shoot you', he continued. Jim could sense the outlaw deciding his next move. With a spring he headed for the water and freedom. Catlike, the warden was on him. Over and over they fought in the mud and water, each man fighting as though his life were at stake.

When the first rays of the sun began to flood the marsh, the poacher was still there but his hands which had so nimbly built the trap and killed the ducks were shackled. Tired, wet and mud covered as he was the warden had caught his man. As usual there was no one around to sing his praises.

'Where are the other wardens?' demanded the handcuffed trapper.

'There's just me', said Jim.

'Tricky one, ain't you?', returned the trapper.

'Takes one to catch one', mused the warden.

THE
SILENT DOG

A mark of the genuine poacher was that he was accompanied by a dog. Usually of unprepossessing appearance this was not just any household pooch but one trained to a high degree and as good, if not better, than the keeper's own shooting dogs. A poacher's dog could start hares and rabbits running to gate-net or long-net, but stop short of pursuing them into it. It was quick enough to pick a hare from a form and bring it back, warn of approaching trouble, be silent at all times, slip home like a shadow when told, make do with very little food and remain loyal to its master unto death.

It risked dog spears, poison, steel and shot from the keeper but it slept by day to be fresh for night work, was companion, foot-warmer, alarm and bag-filler. The loss of a good dog was enough to cause the collapse of many a poaching gang.

THE POACHER'S DOG

A cross between a greyhound and a collie was considered the best, although any sort of mongrel would be pressed into service. Any animal which was capable of snapping up a rabbit where it lay in a hedge bottom couch was deemed good enough, for such was the bread and butter of the wandering moucher's business. However, some poachers' dogs were trained to an astonishing degree. The first cross mentioned combined wisdom with keen sight, speed of foot and excellent scenting powers.

The poacher's dog should never in any circumstances give tongue, no matter how hot the pursuit in which it is engaged. It will search a hedge and start rabbits towards the long net, itself stopping within a yard of the meshes; it should be able to run down a hare and retrieve it to hand, and only break silence to give a low, warning growl at the approach of an unseen stranger. It is directed by the slightest wave of a hand – the poacher will not need to give away his presence by using verbal commands.

The best dogs seemed to enter the spirit of the game, snatching what sleep they could during the day and ever ready for night work. One old training trick was to teach the dog to go home when the traditional 'come here' whistle or call was sounded. Thus a poacher apprehended and commanded to call up his dog would whistle and shout for all he was worth – but the dog had been trained that at that sound it should immediately slink off safely home. The loss of such a dog was a serious blow to a poacher and sometimes to a whole gang; some were put out of business when the dog, the key to the operation, was lost for one reason or another.

The keeper was, of course, ordered to destroy all such dogs at every opportunity but with the proviso that on no account should this risk harming a fox, as many shooting estates preserved their foxes for hunting. Setting snares always involved such a risk, and there were doubtless many accidents which were kept quiet. A snare should be set where paths intersect, at stream crossings, and in similar well-used places; it should be stout, and a bough bent over and pegged so that when the snare was sprung, the victim was half suspended by the branch springing straight. To avoid foxes the keeper would rub the snare and surrounding vegetation with his hands, the human scent deterring a fox but not a dog.

THE PROFESSIONALS

The keeper went to some lengths to discourage tramps, pedlars and strangers from visiting his house. He had discovered that they rarely had good reason for the call and their real motive was to spy out the land and discover the disposition of the keeper and his surroundings. What was more, those with transport, the carriers with horse-drawn closed vans, were often used as smugglers for poached game.

A good keeper therefore kept a savage dog at his gate, taught to bark and growl at strangers. Such a dog could easily be trained by asking genuine visitors to thrust a broom in his face, or even by the keeper himself dressing in rags and acting the part of a vagrant – although I imagine his scent would have given him away.

A Bright Lad

Some poachers were out one night with long dogs after hares. One of the dogs came back clearly in distress and to their horror went into convulsions and died on the spot before their eyes. They felt sure that the keeper had left out a carcase baited with strychnine especially for that purpose.

Later in the day the same men came upon the keeper's little lad on his way to school. The burly leader approached the lad and asked in a wheedling voice: 'Sammy, does your forther use strike-o-nine to poison folk's dogs with?'

'No', said Sammy, skipping a yard further out of range; 'he uses strike-o-ten'. As the old editions of *Punch* used to say, 'Collapse of stout party'.

Night Dog

Then, as now, it was strongly recommended that a keeper should not go on night patrol without the companionship and protection of a suitable dog. A cross between a mastiff and a bulldog was ideal, a creature of natural savagery and tenacity who simply loved nothing more than chasing people and biting them. The dog should be kept muzzled except in cases of extreme emergency – for when loosed without his muzzle he should be a fearsome beast, seeming to wish to make up for all the times he had wanted to bite people in the past but been prevented.

A keeper could train such a dog to chase a poacher and run between his legs, bringing him down. The dog would also warn of miscreants hiding nearby in the bushes, for his keen sense of smell would supplement the sight and hearing of his master; and he could detect the approach of folk in the dark long before a human knew anyone was within a mile of the place.

It did no harm if suitably embroidered tales of the dog's ferocity went round the village. The keeper regularly fuelled this legend with casually dropped 'asides' of the fearful maimings and damage done by his 'little dog' the night before, and of some unfortunate victim languishing in hospital hoping to recover from dreadful wounds. This news would spread swiftly and was further enhanced in the re-telling so the reputation for the man-eating dog became well established.

A bitch was to be preferred to a dog for keeper's companion on night work. For one thing, a bitch could be more savage and relentless than any dog – and there was another reason, which the following yarn will explain:

One estate was blessed with a mastiff dog of such unbelievable ferocity that there was little poaching, for none dared risk facing the brute's jaws. In time the keepers grew complacent, and relied too much on their four-legged friend and his reputation to do their work for them. One night in the peak of shooting season they grew so lax that they left but two men on prowl while they attended a servants' ball in a neighbouring mansion.

The two keepers sauntered down the dark rides, taking little care and depending on the dog to be their eyes, ears and protection. Suddenly they were pounced on by a poaching gang who had lain in wait for them in the bushes. They were tied up into neat parcels with rope and tumbled into a dry ditch, where they suffered the cold comfort of hearing the poachers knocking down numerous birds from the trees. They could not believe what had happened to the mighty dog; he had dashed off in the right direction sure enough, but then mysteriously had seemed to vanish.

Eventually they were rescued, still no sign of the dog, and they concluded that the poachers had poisoned it with baited meat, although no body had been found. The next day, however, they were surprised to see old Titan sleeping in his kennel, none the worse for whatever had happened to him.

It remained a mystery, until later it leaked out that the poachers had come armed with a bitch 'in an interesting condition', and old Titan, preferring love to fighting, had dashed off in pursuit of amour leaving the poachers to carry on undisturbed. Thus, bitches every time, for they do not suffer from such pangs of passion.

A chasing dog would die from self-inflicted wounds on the so-called dog spear

DEALING WITH THE POACHER'S DOG, 1850 STYLE – ACCORDING TO JOHN WILKINS

Take a rabbit's liver, heart and lights and 'season' them. Put them into a pound canister tin and carry the tin in your breast pocket. You will require four livers, or four 'seasoned' doses and you should lay some blood with each dose. Lay one dose two or three yards away from each gate and, while the poacher is engaged in setting his net, the dog will scent the blood on the dose, come up and eat it.

The poacher sets his net and then, not knowing what his dog has been about calls – 'Here Bob, go on, good dog.' Away goes Bob across the field but before he has gone a hundred yards he begins to feel very queer and staggery. He winds a hare and makes a rush for her but, as he is drawing up to her flanks, he pitches a somersault head over heels. He tries to rise but only falls over again, his legs going as stiff as iron pokers.

It is all up with poor Bob, he never returns to his master but lays there until next morning. You come to pick up your doses and find one clean gone. Look about you and you will see a great prize. Put him in a bag and bury him with all honours. That gang of poachers is broken up for the season, for it is a hundred to one that they cannot get another dog and if they do, it won't be another 'Bob' but some animal of very little use to them.

I make my own alarm guns and can set them in the field or woods so as to make the dog commit suicide, but the same drawback applies to this as well as the doses – a fox may get killed as well as a poacher's dog.

THE PLAYFUL DOG

Ian Niall recalls a time when two poachers were saved by the dog who loved a game.

Two friends of mine who were chased by a keeper ran through the park carrying a gun and a sack containing four birds and accompanied by their lurcher. When a second keeper joined the first and a car began to race ahead of them down an adjoining drive, it seemed certain that they would be caught. One swung off and ran at right angles to the original flight and the other turned to give battle. The two keepers separated. The running poacher who carried the sack and gun became the quarry of one of the keepers. The poacher who stood his ground gave a signal to his dog.

It ran in quickly and snapped at the heel of the keeper's boot and over he went. The second keeper hesitated and the poacher broke back past him. He turned to give chase and the lurcher somehow ran in between his legs and brought him down as he had the other. The first poacher was by now well into the shelter of a nearby wood. His companion whistled up the dog and ran on and soon he, too, was in cover. It seemed that the dog had been taught the game by the children of one of them and had become a bugbear in the village for the habit of upending anyone who ran or moved fast. It sobered them both a little when I remarked that it was a good thing the dog had not chosen to turn playful with either of *them* while the keepers were in chase.

The Silent Dog

Lynn Doyle writes in Ballygullion *of Pat Murphy and his friends on a long-netting night on the squire's park. His companions are ill-experienced in the gentle art, and for their purposes they have acquired a 'silent dog' which, in spite of the sternest tests to which they put it, would utter no sound to give away the game.*

'Faith' sez I, 'it's well he's some good points about him for be me sowl he's no beauty.' An' nayther he was; a low set, crooked legged baste wi' a dirty brown coat and a wee bunty tail. Wan av his ears was half tore off an' he'd lost two teeth in the front.

'We couldn't have picked a better night', sez Mr. Anthony. 'We'll be able to see what we're doing.' 'Aye, an' the rabbits'll be able to see what we're doing too,' sez I, 'There's no good startin' till it clouds over a bit.' It was rising a bit cloudy behind the wind an' I knowed the moon would soon be covered. 'Maybe you're right,' sez Mr. Anthony. 'I'll tell you what I'll do while we're waiting. I'll run back an' get the airgun. It'll make no noise an' I might get a shot at a rabbit.'

'If ye take my advice', sez I, 'ye'll let the gun alone'. But he never listened to me, an' made off up the avenue at a trot, lavin' me an' Mr. Barrington standin' there.

After half a mile walk we come to the plantin' below the big house. There's about fifteen acres av it in a sort of half moon, then a big stretch of grass they call the lawn right up to the hall door wi' an odd big tree in it here and there. The upper end av the plantin's fair alive wi' rabbit holes, and av a fine night the rabbits does be feedin' on the lawn in hundreds. Our schame was to run the nets along in front of the holes, an' thin get round an' let the dog loose to scare the rabbits intil them.

As soon as we got the nets set we slipped round the horn av the plantin' close to the house. Mr. Anthony puts the chain he has the dog on in my hand. 'Now Pat', he sez, 'you hould the dog in till we get to the middle av the lawn, and maybe I'll get a shot', sez he, putting a pellet in the airgun.

'Ye auld fool,' thinks I, 'wi' your pop gun; it's well if ye don't lame somebody', for his hands was in such a trimmble wi narvousness that he could hardly snap the breech. Howiver, out we moves, an' just then, as ill luck would have it, out comes the moon. 'Bad cess to ye' sez I, 'ye ould divil ye, weren't ye alright behind there, but ye must come out an spoil sport.'

But Mr. Anthony was well plazed. 'Wheesht, Pat,' sez he; 'I see wan.' Wi' that he puts his foot in a rabbit hole, an' down he slaps on his face, an' the gun snaps and pins the dog in the side somewhere. Maybe it was more than the mortial baste could stan', for thim wee pellets is cruel, but anyway the dog sets up the horridest howlin' ye iver heard, an' I was that taken in that I dropped the chain and let him go.

An' thin the fun begins – Mr. Anthony rippin' and cursin' an' spitting out bits av grass an' the silent dog runnin' round and round wi' the chain rattlin' behind

him like a tinker's cart. 'For a silent dog' sez I, 'he's makin' a brave noise.' 'Shut up ye fool', sez Mr. Anthony, as mad as you like, 'an catch the brute. Be the mortial,' sez he 'if I catch him, I'll make a silent dog av him.'

All av a suddin the big front door opens wi' a clatter. 'Come on men,' I hears old Mr. Hastings' voice. 'Scatter across the lawn an' ye can't miss the blackguards. I can hear their dog.' Ye niver saw three men run faster than we did for that plantin'. 'Look out for the nets,' sez I, but wee Mr. Anthony was runnin' like a redshank ten yards in front of us and niver heard me. The net took him just on the shin bone, an' he riz about two foot in the air, an lit on his belly on the plantin' ditch wi' a sough. Whin we got up to him, he could hardly spake.

'Up wi you quick'; 'I can't,' sez he wi' a groan; 'me heart's busted,' sez he. 'Not a bit av it' sez Mr. Barrington feelin' him, 'it's only your braces.'

(*They escape, and hear the pursuing keepers' cries fading into the distance in pursuit of the 'silent dog' which is still making a fearful noise. The fugitives hear two distant shots, then silence. A week later Mr. Barrington and Pat are down by the river, leaning over the bridge and discussing their recent adventure.*)

Thin I sees something come floating down the river. 'Be the mortial, Mr. Barrington,' sez I, whin I looked at it for a minit, 'it's him.' 'Not a bit av it', sez he; 'it's twice the size.' 'Maybe he's a bit swelled.' sez I; an' whin it floated down the length of the bridge, sure enough, it was himself. Mr. Barrington stands lookin' at him till I war near turned, for in troth he was smellin' higher nor a daisy.

'Come on Pat,' sez he at the last turnin' away. 'I'm sorry the poor baste's killed. I'll send someone down to fish him out and give him a dacint burial.'

'It's all ye can do for him, Mr. Barrington' sez I. 'Rest his sowl, if he has one, though I did lose two good rabbit nets be him, he's a silent dog now, anyway.

CLEAN HEELS

Gil Gaylor, the Gatcombe Park poacher, writes of his experiences. Here he is in a wood at night; he has shot a pheasant in a tree, but has heard a distant dog bark.

It was perhaps the keeper's dog that had barked and for a few minutes I lived in an eternity of suspense. Then, all of a sudden, I heard the heavy tramping of dead leaves some way off. I slipped slowly and quietly from where I stood into a shallow ditch by a hazel thicket.

The keeper passed within twenty yards of me, then paused by an oak tree and stood there, peering into the darkness, listening. Luckily for me he did not have his dog with him. I knew that he had heard the crashing of wings and was waiting for the trespasser to betray his presence.

It was a beautiful, moonlit night and from my hiding place I could see him staring to and fro into the darkness of the hazel thickets. The minutes ticked by, then with a further trampling of leaves the keeper moved away in a different direction. I waited several more minutes, then myself moved cautiously away. The night was finished. The keeper might be going for a dog …

THE SNARE
OF THE FOWLER

As ancient as the Dead Sea Scrolls, the net, snare, hingle or noose – there must be hundreds of local names – is a basic tool of the poacher's trade. Costing nothing and fashioned from the horsehair, willow wands and ash poles he found around him, the evidence could easily be destroyed, while the confiscation or loss of such gear was of no concern.

The net was another essential and the poacher evolved many ways of using it to advantage, be it for hanging from a gate for a hare, stretched out by the woodside for rabbits, for use with ferrets, for dragging over a stubble at night to catch a covey or for taking fish. No one could call himself a poacher until he had mastered the art of the netmaker.

LONG-NETTING

In Victorian times long-netting was the real money-earner; in those days when the rabbit was king and the market for them was eager, the rabbits caught long-netting commanded the best prices because they were clean and unshot. It was a job which called for no little skill and a good dog, and was the curse of the keepers because it entailed wholesale slaughter.

The best sort of night for this work was dark and blustery with a little light rain – not heavy and continuous, as then the rabbits would not feed or venture far from their buries. The net would be fixed at one end along a woodside or hedge at a time of night when the rabbits were feeding and unsuspicious, well out in the field and far from their homes. A second man would walk backwards unrolling the net was he went, until a great length of woodside was covered. Two companions would follow behind him sticking in the ground at fifteen yard intervals a hazel peg two-and-a-half feet in length, and fixing the top edge cord of the net to it.

The net mesh was made to exact dimensions – just large enough for a rabbit travelling at speed to force its head through, but difficult for it to remove it. As many as six nets would be set, each one a hundred yards in length, which will indicate the scale of such an operation, and the great amount of damage it could do to a rabbit population. One man would take up position at one end of the net with his fingers resting lightly on the top cord, instantly ready to react to the vibration of a rabbit hitting the trammels.

If the gang had no dog, the other men (and the operation called for at least three for it to be successful) would make a wide sweep round the field and beat it back to the waiting nets. The rabbits would by lying out feeding, and their first instinct would be to squat and trust to luck that they were not observed; but they feel insecure so far from their holes, and as the beaters approached they would break cover and make a headlong dash for safety, crashing into the net and getting their heads firmly caught in the meshes. The man at the net meanwhile feels the bump as a rabbit hits, slips quickly from his spot, removes it from the net and kills it deftly with a single blow; he then returns swiftly to his position.

Best of all and most effective is the long-netters' dog when it has been trained and has a natural instinct for the work. The dog will scent rabbits that human beaters may have overlooked and start them for home, for there will always be a few rabbits which stay in the form and do not run straightaway. The dog will start the rabbit running and chase it for a distance, but always stop within a few yards of the net and not blunder into it. Such a dog is like gold dust to a long-netting gang.

Those without a dog could resort to other methods of starting the rabbits. The problem on some nights was not so much to drive them as to make them move at all. Without a lurcher to start them on their headlong dash for safety, the poacher needed to call on his ingenuity to find an acceptable second best. Sometimes he would catch a rabbit and take it to the furthest point on the beat and hold it firmly in his hands so that it squealed in alarm; this was often enough to start the other rabbits moving. Alternatively – but far more risky – he could strike a match from time to time; this would also have the desired effect, but was considered highly dangerous as any night watchers would see the sparks of light in a second and hasten to the spot.

Another way was for the beaters to take a long cord with lead weights attached to it at intervals. Holding one end each they would trail this through the grass or stubble and this would effectively disturb the rabbits. This system was less successful on ground studded with bushes or whins. Instead of lead weights, small sleigh bells could used, or a handful of stones in a cocoa tin, in short, anything which would alarm the squatting rabbits sufficiently to start them moving.

Hares were hardly every caught in this method for the hare makes straight for open ground when disturbed; but sometimes a fox would rush forward and crash into the net causing some degree of upset and bad language as it would have to be set from scratch again.

PREVENTING LONG-NETTING

The keeper could sometimes set alarm guns, but these were not popular on fields where cattle were grazing or near the coverts where pheasants might be roosting. The observant keeper could tell if he was being long-netted simply by the sudden decrease in the number of rabbits in particular fields and by tell-tale signs on the grass. He might release a number of tame rabbits coloured black or piebald on vulnerable fields; their sudden and unexplained absence would tell him immediately that the long-netters had paid him a visit – the best poacher in the world could not distinguish between a common rabbit and a coloured one on a dark night.

It was rare for even the most careful gang to leave without forgetting at least one hazel peg – a sure giveaway. On dewy nights their tracks would be clear in the grass and in frosty weather their footprints were obvious, standing out stark and black against the pale background.

There was another ingenious measure which could be taken to prevent long-netting, but it was applicable only to those grass fields which lay along the covertside and where the landlord owned them; this was to buy a draft of rough hill bullocks of Welsh or Scottish strain. They should be fed late and their hay laid out in a long line by the woodside; they would spend the best part of the night eating it and then lie down nearby to sleep. On the arrival of the netting gang later on, the bullocks might think that here was more food on its way for them and rush up madly to the gang, giving it no peace but bellowing loudly. The men might try to drive them off, but the general commotion would be more than enough to scare any rabbit which had not lost its sense of hearing.

If the poachers had a dog with them this would add to the chaos, for cattle will not leave a dog alone but will chase it hither and thither. If the nets happened to be down already the beasts would rush through them, entangling their legs and effectively wrecking the whole set-up. A crafty poacher would cut a truss of hay from a nearby stack, lead the bullocks to a far corner of the field and when they were quiet, resume business as before. However, not all poachers were so resourceful and there was not always a convenient rick for the purpose.

As in trail-netting, a bunch of scrubby thorns scattered along the probable line where a net would be set would cause great annoyance. However, unlike trail-netting, long-netting was a more careful and circumspect business, and an experienced team would send a spare man crawling in front of the net layer to feel and find the bushes with his hands, and throw them well away from its path. In counter ploy the keepers would sometimes peg the bushes securely to the ground; this would give the poachers more trouble, although it would not stop them entirely. Short, sharp thorns strewn liberally on the ground were as good a remedy as any, for they made the progress of the crawling man a matter of some discomfort.

The other drawback to bushing – which was, after all, only a moderate deterrent – was that the very presence of lines of cut scrub would indicate to all passers-by that this was a field full of rabbits, well worth a visit with the long-net.

Some estates discovered that bean straw was even better than thorns; it was easily obtainable and could be strewed thickly, and would cause great trouble in the net. Also when bone-dry and rotten it made a fearful racket when you walked on it, and thus would alarm every rabbit on the field long before the net was in place.

An inbuilt drawback to long-netting was the fact that because of the rabbits' feeding habits, it had to take place within the same hour or two at night. The most likely period was shortly after chucking-out time at the local ale-house, or between then and dawn. Any keeper knew it was always possible for his estate to be the second in line for a raid, should the netters have bad luck at their first choice, so he could not be pin-point accurate in his estimations; but he could have a fair guess to within an hour or two.

Therefore at about 11 o'clock at night the keeper would go out with a brace of fast terriers and thoroughly beat the ground which he thought the poachers would tackle. The rabbits would be driven safely into their holes, and even if the netters arrived shortly after, they would not by then have ventured so far out again into the field. After a few nights of this regular disturbance the keeper would find that his rabbits would feed more often by day and would not go so far out into the fields. In this way the netters could be successfully thwarted.

BAGGING THE NETTERS

A netting gang usually numbered five people, and the keeper was advised not to tackle them himself but to wait until he could command a team to outnumber them by at least two, ie seven stout-hearted chaps. The idea was to come on the gang when they were all assembled, not when in the act of netting when they would be spread at their various posts about the field. The gang would certainly be armed with stout sticks, and stones were usually ready to hand, so a concerted attack at a single moment was believed to be the most effective.

The watchers should hide near a spot the netters were certain to visit and, each man leaving room for his neighbour to operate, leap out as one. If possible the net should be bagged, as such an item was expensive and the key to the whole operation; without it the gang was lost, and it would take some time and expense to make a replacement.

If the poachers were alarmed and given time to arrange their defence, things could grow ugly – they might form a hollow square like a military operation and hurl flints or stones. The advice in this situation was for each keeper to remove his coat and to wrap half of it around his arms allowing the tail to hang down, thus forming a shield which would take the venom out of the missiles. They should then organise a swift and concerted charge and hand out to the poachers the same sauce intended for them.

On the darkest of nights there was one more way which could be used to break up a poaching gang of netters. With a stout rope about forty yards long, two fast and powerful men would take an end each and run as fast as they could for the poachers, passing them one on each side. The rope should be tightly stretched and held at about knee height. In the dark the poachers were naturally concerned about the whereabouts of their assailants; trying to see where they were, they probably would not spot the rope racing towards them with deadly intent – with luck it would take them at the knee and throw them down in complete confusion. The rope runners should then return with their backup team and secure the gang. However, keepers at all times were advised to take care when tackling poachers who could be as desperate as rats when cornered, known sometimes to throw dust and handfuls of lime into the faces of their attackers.

Good advice was always to call on the men to surrender before wading in with the first blow, and only to attack if they refused and showed fight. However, most poachers would throw in the towel if they realised they were confronted by determined men who outnumbered them. A surrender was far to be preferred to an uncertain affray in a moonlit woodland or stubble field.

PARTRIDGE NETTING

The partridge has never lent itself to poaching as, unlike the pheasant, it prefers open places and roosts away from cover in the safety of fields. However, it was vulnerable to a shot from a poacher's crazy open-bored muzzle-loader with its wide spread of shot and open pattern; and although pheasants with their proclivity to woods and enclosed places offered a better target, partridges were very common in those days and commanded a good price.

The way to come among them was by means of a trail- or trammel-net. This could be of any length depending on the number of men available to work it, but measured between twelve and fifteen feet in width with a bamboo pole at each narrow end. It was carried by two men who would hold the poles at an angle so that the net ran along at an angle to the ground, the leading edge at waist height and the trailing edge brushing the ground behind. The net was made of fine thread or preferably silk, and the trailing edge took the form of a fringe which brushed in the stubble.

A whole covey could be covered in this way, and when the net was dropped, one man would keep hold of his pole whilst his companions carefully knelt down and removed the birds from its meshes. The operation was silent and hard to detect, although tell-tale signs that netters had been out were scattered feathers and toe- and heel-marks on the scuffed ground – but even then it called for a sharp-eyed keeper to spot them.

A good trail-netter spent much time in observation. He would spend many days watching the stubbles to see where the birds 'jugged' for the night – the strident calling of an old cock bird would indicate where they were, and he would

find the little piles of droppings which showed where a covey had settled overnight. The birds also gave away their whereabouts by arriving with a great clatter of wings, and would usually stay near to where they alighted. The poacher would bait the field with bird seed and dari, and this would draw the birds from great distances.

Partridges were especially fond of the last stand of corn left by the reapers. In those pre-combine days the harvest was a protracted affair, and many farms would have swathes of corn which remained uncut until well into autumn. This was a haven for game of all kinds, which came for food. When netting standing corn the poacher adapted his net to include a series of short cords on the trailing edge,

each with a lead weight attached; this would help keep the net close to the ground in the tall crop. Even then it was not easy to drop the net firmly enough on a covey, for it could not be pressed down securely and birds would escape through the sides where the corn prevented the net from touching the earth.

Sheaves of corn were another draw and also a good place for snaring, while in cold weather the birds came to feed in stackyards and anywhere where stock was kept. This gave the farm labourer a chance to have a quick shot with the crow-scaring gun, or to set snares in likely places. The poacher was a stranger to close seasons, and even in the breeding season would snap up any trifles which came his way. For example, in the spring the cock partridge is very belligerent, calling loudly and proclaiming his territory and his new wife to all who can hear. A skilled man can imitate the call, and this would make the little cock come running like the wind to repel what he imagined to be an intruder. The poacher would wait in ambush until the bird came close, and shoot it on the ground, pocket it and make a swift departure from the scene. The keeper might hear the shot, but this was the time of year when the bird scarers were most busy and he would pay it little heed.

Another fruitful time for the opportunist was when the piles of muck were left in neat rows along the fallow fields before being ploughed in. These were full of all sorts of insects and hence very attractive to game, especially in hard weather when food was scarce. It was an easy matter to set traps or horsehair snares or 'sniggles' round the heaps, with a good chance of picking up a bird or two.

HIDING THE NETS

Only the most wealthy could afford the non-bulky, all-but-perfect nets made of silk, and the coarse and more commonly used variety were hard to conceal. Often they needed to be taken home for repair, or moved to another location, and the trick here was for a thin poacher to wind a hundred yards of string netting about his body and wear an overcoat on top. Thus as a moderately bulky poacher he could pass by all but those who knew him well. On arrival at the covert side he would lie on the ground and his pals would unroll him to retrieve their net and operations could begin.

BUSHES

The keeper had one simple and failsafe solution to the trail-netter; he could bush the fields. For this he would use a large clump of bramble, or bunches of blackthorn or whitethorn cut at the time when the prickles stand out at right angles to the stalk. The pieces need not be huge, and they should not be stuck into the ground because the poacher would feel the resistance immediately and remove the obstacle.

The trick was for the bushes to be loose and unobtrusive so that the poachers would drag their net along to the headland ignorant of what they had picked up. The net would roll the prickles over and over, and at every turn they would become more lovingly entangled in the fine mesh until almost all the net was inextricably caught up. To remove such obstructions in the dark was all but impossible; even in full daylight it might take three patient men at least an hour's work and much bad language. This would put an end to operations for that night, and if the field had been generously bushed the poachers would deem it not worth their while to come to that place again.

In modern times the trail-net is still used, often in fields of short sugar-beet. A farmer could always tell when he had been 'done' because the beet was lying in neatly swept rows, alternately this way and that like a newly mown lawn. If the beet had many 'bolts' in it it was hard to net and usually safe, but if the farmer was worried he would bush the fields in the usual way. The traditional thorn bunches were safest; one farmer thought he would go one better and use iron stakes hammered into the ground at intervals – these would surely tear the net and make it unusable. Unfortunately he forgot where he had left his traps and the sugar-beet harvester picked up two of them, with disastrous consequences to the machinery.

HOW TO BEAT THE GATE NETTER

Good advice from John Wilkins in the nineteenth century.

To prevent gate-netting you should tar the lowest rail of the gate, so that when the hare goes underneath it she smears her back. She will then avoid the gate in future and find some other way in and out of the field, for whichever way a hare comes into a field at night, she will go out the same way if she possibly can. Now the hares thus driven to avoid the gate make through the hedges and the more runs there are through the hedges the more chances there are for the hares and the less for the poachers.

THE LONG NET

From Alfred Curtis – a 'proper' poacher of the 1960s.

We put up the old net fifteen yards from the hedge. Syd went out into the field to drive the rabbits with the aid of a tin can full of pebbles on a string dragged behind him.

And then striffing through the grass, the rabbits came. I heard the first one hit the net. I ran to it. Nothing there! Another came and another. I swore I could see them. There were more; they hit the net, I heard them strike it and hither and thither I ran and had never even the tail of a rabbit in my fingers. I was chasing phantoms of rabbits.

Alastair came running up with Syd. 'What's the bag?' 'Nothing! They've been here but I can't catch them.' And with the coming of the grey dawn we saw: the net was punched full of holes where the rabbits had gone through. Our fine net that had looked so strong was completely rotten.

REVENGE!

A clear ten days I gave those rabbits to forget then off I set again for Lady Eaton's with Syd to help me once more. There was no call for the string and can as I had

brought Brinnie with me. We put up the new net and my fingers were glad at the sound strength of it. I whispered to Brinnie: 'Go! Find 'em boy!'

He vanished in the vast shadow that was night over the field. We waited. A rabbit came thrumming on the ground. It came, it thudded into the net and Brinnie followed. We heard it squeal, and now there was no need for Brinnie to drive, for at the sound all the rabbits in the field bolted for home. The net was suddenly jerking, alive with leaping forms and not one rabbit went through.

There was no time for orthodox killing; we ran up and down punching and slaughtering as fast as we could. Forty five rabbits in less than half an hour. How many poachers, I wonder, can say better than that? It took us several journies working together till at last nets and rabbits were hidden safely in a little spinney. We made a little fire to keep alive the warmth we had acquired and brewed tea. It seemed scarcely half an hour before we saw the streaks of dawn in the sky and the sky paling through the trees: we should have to work fast.

And fast we did work at gutting rabbits. We'd hang one up, split it from vent to chest with our knives that were as sharp as razors, grab it with forelegs and hind, throw it back over the left shoulder and cast – and out, of their own weight, came all the entrails into the bushes.

We sold them for sixpence each – always provided we might have back the pelt, for rabbit skins were sometimes worth more than the meat in those days.

KENZIE

A time warp moves us from the wild men of the turn of the century, to one of the best known poachers who ever lived: the sturdy form of McKenzie ('Kenzie') Thorpe of Sutton Bridge. He was of Romany stock, and his formidable grandmother – magnificently named Leviathan – could, they said, whip up a sitting pheasant, eggs and all, into her apron before the bird could squeak.

Kenzie started in a way his Victorian ancestors would have recognised as a bird-starver, equipped with a rusty old muzzle-loader.

His first, second and third 'proper' guns he stole. They were of a type known loosely as 'farm guns', kept in barns for shooting rats or pigeons and of no great value; but for Kenzie the price was right and he used them to start on what turned out to be an illustrious career. As a teenager he got to know the ways of the fen spinneys and the pheasants that roosted there, learning quickly to discriminate between the silhouette of a pheasant, a magpie and a pigeon. Hares, rabbits and game of all sorts made its way to the Thorpe household, shortly followed by the local policeman who was to beat a well-worn path to their front door in the years that followed.

The series of stolen guns ended when Kenzie actually bought his first legitimate weapon; this was a .410, good enough for a start, but it lacked the power he needed so he soon changed it for a single-barrel 12-bore. He went where he wished and would come home loaded with wildfowl, pheasants and hares. He was a remarkable caller of hares, and this trick he demonstrated to millions on one of the several television programmes made about him, so that all could see how it worked. In fact there was no reason why the call should have been successful, for hares make no sound to resemble it. He had inherited the trick from his gypsy forebears. The noise is a peculiar moaning sucking of the lips which rises in intensity and volume, and when any hare hears it, it will pop up its ears in the corn and come lolloping to the place as though drawn by a magnet.

ESCAPING FLOSSIE

Kenzie was calling hares, hiding in a dyke and drawing the hares to him. Two approached and he knocked them both down; he called again and two more appeared in the distance, heading towards him. But at that moment he saw a black figure approaching down the bank, Flossie Longlands, the owner of the estate and a lady blessed with a fair turn of speed.

'I flew out, grabbed the hares, and ran back to the bank. I pretended to go east, but doubled back and went west, ran down the bank and nipped along the ditch at the bottom, and at last I threw her off. But when I got back to the boat it had tipped over with the falling tide and sunk. It took me three-quarters of an hour to bale her out – then I loaded the gun and the hares in her, and rowed across the river so that Flossie could not get to me and I walked two miles home.'

Such was a fairly typical day in his life, strenuous and with no respect for property; but it was an effective bag-filler, and he was no stranger to hard work.

NABBED

Kenzie was caught many times in his career, once spending a spell in Norwich prison for a 'do' with a keeper; on this particular occasion he was out with a pal Arthur Porter in his timber lorry, enjoying a poaching safari through the Norfolk lanes, armed with a double-barrelled .410. In a field between Kings Lynn and Holt, Kenzie saw six pheasants all together; he 'gave them one', and stuffed three of them under the lorry seat. Two miles more and they saw another batch; two others joined the three beneath the seat. Almost into Heacham and he dropped another brace.

Then the law in the shape of the local bobby appeared, and stood his ground even when threatened to be run down by the lorry. There was a fight for possession of the .410 which Kenzie lost. The case came up at Kings Lynn, and Kenzie appeared in a dressing gown, old flannel trousers and carpet slippers; he was fined seven pounds and the loss of the gun. His travelling expenses in war-time with petrol rationing were sixteen shillings and Arthur got off with a pound. It was an expensive 'do' and all the gratitude Arthur showed was to buy Kenzie a single pint of mild beer at fourpence and he did not even say 'thank-you'.

TERRINGTON MARSH

Inside the sea wall at Terrington was a newly reclaimed marsh which was a haven for roosting pheasants. Kenzie poached this regularly in spite of several run-ins with the venerable custodian of the place, who concluded that he had met his match. However, Kenzie decided that the place was being used by too many other locals so he organised a mass poach-in.

Running it as a parody of the squire's 'posh' shoot, he had his flanking guns and

beaters and they started to drive the first hundred-acre bay. They were shooting many birds and hares when Kenzie realised that there was another rival gang at the other end of the bay doing exactly the same as he. His lot kept going until old Watson the keeper and some assistants added themselves to the opposition, and came in hot pursuit. Kenzie came to a wide creek against the bank of which was fastened an old punt fixed to a rope which Watson habitually used as a ferry to take himself to and fro.

Kenzie's party crossed on this punt in relays, the last batch arriving safely as old Watson came puffing up, threatening goodness knows what vengeance. Kenzie did no more than raise his gun and blow the bottom out of the boat, leaving his antagonists with a two-mile slog round the outside before they could catch up with him. Not deterred, Kenzie and his 'shoot' continued with their sport on the other side of the water.

'And that's how it was in those days, poaching all over, going where I liked and doing what I liked. And the rougher the weather the better. That's how it was. We was chased and I was chased, hundreds of times, but we was never caught and nor was I, not until we got into the nineteen-forties. But that was the cream of it, round about 1928.'

MIXED BAGS FOR HARD TIMES

In the war, rationing made meat a rare commodity and Kenzie shot anything on wings which bore a scrap or two of flesh and was, therefore, negotiable. He conveyed his week's bag on a rusty wheelbarrow to an eager market in the town, and the contents of that vehicle would have given birdwatchers as well as gastronomes quite a shock. It included Brent geese, shelduck, gulls of various sorts, ruffs and reeves, waterhens, black-tailed godwits as well as the more conventional rabbits, hares, pheasants, partridges and mallard.

His cartridges were supplied by the RAF – though without their knowing much about it – who kept a supply for training pilots in air gunning. He probably wasted fewer than they did.

THE RECORD YEAR

A bumper year was 1942. Kenzie had been declared unfit for military service due to an old wound picked up in a family fracas. His bag was as follows: September, 77 head, mostly partridges and hares. October, 108 head including 15 mallard, 9 wigeon, 24 partridges, and 18 pheasants. November, 185 head including 76 mallard, 72 wigeon, 7 geese. December, 183 head, a mixed bag of 81 pheasants, 40 geese, 52 wigeon and 20 shelduck. January produced 146 wigeon, 25 geese, 43 shelduck, 11 curlew, the total for the month being 257 head. February concluded this marathon with 45 geese, 137 shelduck, 65 wigeon, 15 mallard, 2 curlew, 1 hare and 1 swan.

The total for this amazing year was 1,044 head to his own gun.

An Embarrassing Moment

Kenzie was taking out shooters fairly regularly and had gained a considerable reputation as a guide of rare quality and character. The young Peter Scott learned his fowling with Kenzie, as did many other gentleman gunners of the period. On one of these outings Kenzie had with him two gentlemen used to the finer things in life, one being a recent Lord Lieutenant of his county, the other a considerable landowner. They recalled that Kenzie took them to a shed where he kept his gear, though they were not allowed so much as a peep inside. However, one of them craned his neck at an impossible angle and did manage to catch a glimpse inside as Kenzie slid through the quarter-opened door: the walls were lined with pheasants hanging up and ready for market. Not one of them, we may fairly guess, had been come by legitimately.

They were out shooting geese on a stubble in conditions of low ground-mist. They had had a number of shots when Kenzie spotted two legs approaching through the murk, and leaped out of his dyke yelling 'Run boys! here comes the keeper!' Those two highly respected men, JPs and pillars of respectability both, were obliged to flee across the muddy field, bags flapping and red in the face, to escape from the legitimate wrath of the gamekeeper. At home, each employed his own keeper; but as usual Kenzie was unrepentant, and offered no apology.

Folk learned to take Kenzie at his own valuation of himself.

Swan Downing

The demand for fresh meat in those times of severe rationing caused Kenzie and his pal Horry Savage to stretch the rules. Swans there were in hundreds in the Lincolnshire fens, and the odd one had been well received by the game dealer. Kenzie and Horry therefore cycled the sixteen miles to Spalding, where they fell in with a good herd of mute swans. Armed with a .410 they knocked out seven of them, packed three into one bag and four in another, and set off home. On the long road they came across another swan sitting by the verge; Kenzie took his torch, dazzled the bird and shot that one, too. Without doubt they were, as Kenzie would say, 'ver, ver warm' when they arrived back at Sutton Bridge.

ROYAL POACHING

Kenzie's most audacious feat was to poach the royal covers at Sandringham with his friend Horry Savage. Armed with a .22 rifle and the .410 and driving an Austin 7, the pair were afterwards stopped by Mr Amos, the king's keeper, and an underkeeper. There ensued a sort of wrestle for the possession of the gun and a cock pheasant which lay under the seat. Kenzie was outnumbered two to one and eventually bested, for Horry was no fighting man; and to make matters worse, the trusty car – which till then had removed them in the nick of time from many a potentially difficult situation – failed to start, and both were fairly nabbed.

The subsequent summons included confiscation of rifle, £1 for possession of a firearm without a certificate, £5 for coming from land in pursuit of game, £4 for trespassing and £1 for opposing a constable, for Amos was a 'Special'.

THE SLAMMER

Kenzie had appeared often enough at Holbeach Magistrates' Court for them to be heartily sick of him. When in 1945 he attacked a keeper and knocked him down he was convicted of grievous bodily harm and sent to Norwich prison for three months. This was a gruelling experience, but one which he survived unscathed; I have a clear picture of him gazing out over the walls and seeing a troop of green plover wailing by, high on their club wings. At that moment his situation struck him most forcibly, this free spirit used to roaming where and when it wished being condemned to a spell behind bars.

He was not reformed by the experience and continued to poach the large farms near his village, only abandoning the long trips to less familiar country.

KENZIE ON POACHING

'You've got to be as cunning as a fox to outwit the keepers, farmers and labourers and anyone who lives inside your poaching area. You have to keep your ears and eyes open: notice any little sight and sound you have never heard or seen before. You've got to know your ground, your ditches, your roadways on which a car can approach at night without its headlights. You've got to know every bush, tree, every haystack. If there's a new object sticking up from a dyke or bank you must investigate it before you start work. If you don't you will be nervous, and this will put you off. At night don't think of starting until every light has gone out and everything is still.

'Outwitting a gamekeeper can be very simple if you stick to the rules. You've got to know his whereabouts, his movements, his habits and the company he keeps. Does he visit pubs? Does he have regular cronies? If he has, then with a bit of luck you've got him for you know where he'll be at certain times.

'Stay clear of estates with several keepers because they can run a duty rosta like the army, and keep guard four on and four off. Keep an eye on the keeper's cottage when you're out at night.

'And when you're out in the fields at night, have a shot here and a shot there with a .410 gun. That way they'll never catch up with you. Once you're on the job, keep to the fields and dykes and never cross a road. Never go near a cottage for, no matter if you're walking like a cat, some dog will give you away with his "yap, yap". And no matter how successful you've been, never visit the same place two nights running. If they know the place has been poached they'll be watching for poachers again – but they won't catch you if you're working five miles away on a different farm.'

Torching

'One of my favourite ways of operating at night has always been to take the roosting pheasants out of trees with a .22 rifle. Try to spot the birds without using the light; there may be as many as ten birds in one tree. If there's a good wind blowing and the night is rough you can sometimes get all of those pheasants without any trouble at all. The method is this: first show your torch on the ground. You look up and find your first bird with the naked eye – then straightaway cock your torch onto it and shoot, but leave it where it falls. You drop your torch again and switch off. Pick your next bird by the naked eye, too, then up with the rifle and repeat the performance. Don't move between shots; stand dead still and the birds won't take fright. I've had nine cocks out of nine in one tree, never picking the birds up until I'd knocked them all down.

'When I dussent use a torch for any reason I'd go round the trees with a .410 gun; this allows you to be just that bit more inaccurate. I use short cartridges loaded with number six shot. You aim by running your gun up the tree and firing directly the barrel blots out the bird.'

TORCHING ON GRASS

Kenzie would torch on short grass or stubble, and also on ploughed land, again using the .22. The best weather for this was severe snow, rainstorms and gales. The poacher had to walk into the wind with the torch strapped onto the bottom of the rifle, sweeping it from left to right to about ten degrees either side of the line of march. Walking very slowly he would never pass a bird and they would sit very tight; at times Kenzie had five or six pheasants 'jugging' within a few yards of him. Without moving he could get them all, unless one of them was wounded and started fluttering on the ground, in which case it would put the rest of them up.

However, the startled birds would rarely fly far, but would probably settle again in the same field so they could be attended to later. Walking at the correct pace, one man could cover a forty-acre field in about three hours. To take up to fifty pheasants in a night by this method was not uncommon; and that is a great weight of birds to carry, calling for more than one trip to take them off the field.

TORCHING HARES

Hares could be torched, but were harder work than pheasants or partridges which would sit and be slaughtered fairly tamely. For hares you worked at far greater range, about fifty or sixty yards compared with five or ten for birds. A powerful torch was needed, and when you spotted a hare in the form you swing the beam off her straightaway. Let it linger on her for even a few seconds and she would be up and away, scaring all the other pheasants and hares in her dash to get away. Swing slowly back to her, taking aim as you do so, and shoot the moment you can 'draw a bead' on her.

CALLING HARES

Kenzie made the most of his remarkable ability to 'call' hares, using that strange, wailing cry which it seemed they could not resist. 'In the spring of the year I've stood in the middle of a grass field in pitch darkness and called hares all around me. I've knocked over seven or eight in five minutes. You call the hares across the field and then put the torch on them and, believe me, you can get them as easy as pie when you know how.'

Especially good times for him were the nights of full moon during February or March, hiding in a dyke armed with a 12-bore by a field of young wheat, for favourite. Sometimes they would come too fast to be killed, a swift right and left and barely time to reload before the next couple were on him – he once had eighteen hares from one dyke in little over an hour, without himself moving. Even he did not know why they came for his call, for it was unlike any cry made by hares – which are usually mute, except when wounded.

TRAIL-NETTING

We have investigated the Victorian method of trail-netting; it was an effective system then, and Kenzie was not the only East Anglian to use it later on. It suited the large, treeless fields where game birds roosted on the ground. Kenzie's net was fourteen yards by thirteen with the usual pole at each end, top and bottom lines and made of four-inch diamond mesh, or even better, four-inch square mesh (birds tended to become less tangled in square mesh than in diamond).

Carried at the customary ten degrees to the ground, the right-hand man had left hand forward, right hand down, the second chap the other way round. You laid the net on the stubble and the right-hand man took charge; poor communication meant tangles, and tangles meant a waste of time and much profanity, and in extreme cases the end of the night's work. The leader gave a twitch on his net as a sign to move, and off you went. When a bird sprang you felt a pluck, both dropped the net instantly, one man running to the front, the other to the back. The bird was removed, each returned to his pole, a twitch on the net and off you went again.

When you got to the end of the field you gave a pull on the net which made your mate stop immediately, two more pulls and he wheeled round you, one pluck and you were ready for the next swathe; in this way you combed the whole field.

'One night in a clover field with Horry a thick haze come over. It was very frosty and you could see your tracks so you could keep nice, straight paths up and down the field. We was catching pheasants galore. The pheasants were that worried by the mist that they wouldn't get up. Some of them were letting the net go right over them. One particular time when we dropped the net we took the pheasants out and Horry took a step forward and put his foot on another cock just sitting on the stubble, and we caught that one, too. The pheasants were getting up and going down in the same field. They was properly scared that night, and we was properly scared, too, because we were catching so many. We took forty-three pheasants and four partridge that night, and we'd only done a quarter of the field.'

The modern antidote for the trail-netter was exactly the same as it was a century ago: the keeper who bushed the field or peppered it with stakes could keep the netters at bay. Kenzie abandoned trail-netting in the end, despite the great success he had with it over the years.

'We packed up trail-netting in the end. Hiding the poles was the trouble. Once we hid them in a tunnel, and the floods came up and floated them out and they were found. Another time we hid them in a wheat-straw stack, and we went by there one day and they'd started stripping the stack and we saw the poles laying out on the ground, so we lost that lot. And a third set we put in a straw stack that went on fire – so we packed up. It was a very exciting business, trail-netting, but we liked to feel free, and not have to worry about finding our gear.'

A PHILOSOPHICAL VIEW

Kenzie Thorpe was an original, a rare bird treated with suspicion by keepers and landowners but one who occupies a niche in folklore as a man with rare skills; a man who cared little for authority, and who despite the strait-jacket of modern civilisation, lived the life of an untamed spirit. As time passed he 'became respectable' and established himself as a wildfowling guide. He became fêted as a conservationist, took films of seals on the Wash, and appeared on TV and radio. However, I like to think that society never tamed him and that underneath the new veneer the old Kenzie still lurked, as wicked and unrepentant as ever.

A wonderful biography of Kenzie has been written by Colin Willock; it is entitled *Kenzie The Wild Goose Man* and may already be fairly termed a classic of field sports literature. I acknowledge this book with gratitude as the source of some of the Kenzie poaching adventures I have described. The last word on Kenzie and poaching I leave with the man himself.

'I have to admit that sometimes, afterwards, especially when I've been caught, I felt very, very ashamed of poaching. But I'd soon forget it when I got a gun in my hands again and a pocketful of cartridges and was out among the pheasants. It wasn't the money I made from it. All told I paid out £150 in poaching fines and I lost four good guns. Apart from that I used to give quite a few of the hares and stuff away. I'm not denying, mind, that I made quite a bit from my birds as well. But it wasn't the money at all, it was the sheer thrill of it. And I know if I had my time over again I wouldn't do it any different, except I'd be more cunning about it and I wouldn't go walking up a man's birds on a Sunday morning, which I used to do for the pure daring of it. I'd be a lot more cunning.'

BURNING
THE WATER

Many were the differences between the Scottish and English poacher, the former being held to be a far nobler creature. Not for him the night creeping in the woods but a mob-handed, frontal attack on the salmon river with boats, needle-sharp leisters, flaming cressets of tarred pine, wild Gaelic songs, many a dram of malt and silvery threshing of monster salmon as they were hauled over the thwarts.

Methods of fish poaching had not the variety of those for winged or furred game, but the snatching hook, net or even leister are considered if not acceptable then at least understandable, whereas for the thugs who kill a whole stretch of river with poison for the few salmon that are in it, a blow from which it takes the water many seasons to recover, there is universal loathing among both keeper and genuine poacher.

FISH POACHING

From The Amateur Poacher *by Richard Jefferies.*

There is a way of fishing with rod and line, but without a bait. The rod should be in one piece and stout, the line also very strong but short, the hook of large size. When a fish is discovered the hook is quietly dropped into the water and allowed to float along until close under it. The rod is jerked up and the barb enters the body of the fish and drags it out.

This plan requires, of course, that the fish should be visible, and is more easily practised if it is stationary, but it is also effective against small fish that swim in large shoals, for if the hook misses one it strikes another. The most fatal time for fish is when they spawn; roach, jack and trout alike are then within reach, and if the poacher dares to visit the water he is certain of a haul.

SCROPE'S SNEAK FISHER

Days and Nights of Salmon Fishing *was a minor classic written in 1898 by William Scrope; it described salmon fishing on the Tweed, the strange characters who pursued that sport, and often their poaching tricks, in the days when salmon were plentiful but still jealously preserved. The throwing spear or leister was the favourite weapon, but a cunning man resorted to other tricks.*

Your plausible poacher and river sneak sallies forth with apparent innocence of purpose; he switches the water with a trout rod and ambulates the shore with a small basket at his back indicative of humble pretensions but has a pocket in his

jacket that extends the whole breadth of the skirts. He is trouting forsooth, but ever and anon, as he comes to a salmon cast, he changes his fly and has a go at the nobler animal. If he hooks a salmon, he looks on each side with the tail of his eye to guard against surprise and if he sees any danger of discovery from the advance of the foeman he breaks his line, leaves the fly in the fish's mouth and substitutes the trout one – said fish swims away and does not appear in evidence.

I once came upon one of these innocents who had hold of a salmon with this trout rod in a cast a little above Melrose Bridge called the Quarry Stream. He did not see me for I was in the copsewood on the summit of the bank immediately behind him. I could have pounced on him at once, I and my fisherman. Did I do so? I tell you no. He would have broken his line as above and lost the fish; and I wanted a salmon for it is a delicate animal and was particularly scarce at that time.

So I desired Charlie to lie down amongst the bushes and not to stir till the fish was fairly landed and was in the capacious pocket, which was already described. Then I counselled him to give chase and harry the possessor. Judging, however, that if the man crossed the river at the ford a little below, which he was very likely to do, that he would have so much law of Charlie before he could descend the steep brae that he might escape, I drew back cautiously, got into the road out of sight and passed over Melrose Bridge taking care to bend my body so as to keep it out of sight behind the parapet. I then lay concealed on the opposite bank.

Thus we had master sneak between us. I was at some distance from the scene of the action to be sure and somewhat in the rear, as I could advance no further under cover, but I had the upper ground and was tolerably swift of foot in those days which gave me confidence. I took out my pocket glass and eyed my man. He was no novice, but worked his fish with great skill. At length he drew him onto the shore and gave him a settler with the rap of a stone on the back of his head. He then, honest man, pried around him with great circumspection, and seeing no one he took the salmon by the tail and, full of internal contentment, deposited it in his well-contrived pocket. He then waded across to the south side of the river with the intention, as it seemed, of revisiting his household gods and having a broil.

Charlie now arose form his lair and scrambled down the steep. The alarm was given but he of the salmon had a good start with the river between him and his pursuer. So he stops for a moment on the haugh to make out what was going forward on all sides, much after the fashion of an old hare who runs a certain distance when she apprehends anything personal, she rests for a moment or two and shifts her ears in order to collect the news from all quarters of the compass.

Even so did our friend and having satisfied himself that he was a favoured object of attention he was coy and took to flight incontinently. I now sprang up from the firs for the game was fairly afoot and kept the upper ground. The pursuit came close and hot but as the fugitive like Johnny Gilpin carried weight, I soon closed with him.

'You seem in a hurry my good friend; your business must be pressing. What makes you run so?' 'Did ye no see that bogle there by the quarry stream that garred me rin this gait; haud on for our lives sir for if he overtakes us we are deid men.' 'Why, the truth is, Sandy, that I do not choose to haud on at present because I came in quest of a bonny salmon and cannot go home without one. Could you not help with me such a thing?'

At this, Sandy took a pinch of snuff from his mull and seeing my eyes fixed upon the length and protuberance of his pocket, answered quaintly enough; 'Ay, that I can, and right glad am I to do ye a favour: ye shall no want a salmon whilst I have one.'

So saying he pulled forth a ten pounder, which occupied all the lower regions of his jacket. 'How the beast got in there' said he as he extracted him gradually, 'I dinna ken, but I am thinking that he must have louped intill my pocket as I war wading the river.'

THE THROWING LEISTER

This throwing leister is used chiefly on the upper parts of the Tweed and its tributary streams where the water is not deep. The spear has five prongs of unequal but regularly graduated length, those which are nearest the fisherman and which come to the ground first in throwing being the shortest. The entire iron frame of the spear is double the weight of that in common use. An iron hoop is bound round the top of the pole as a counterbalancing weight and the pole itself has a slight curve, the convex part being the outermost in throwing. A rope made of goat's hair called 'the lyams' is fastened to the bar of the spear just above the shortest prong. This rope is about twelve yards long and is tied to the arm of the thrower. The spear is cast like a javelin and if thrown by a skilful hand, the top of the shaft, after it has pierced the fish, falls beyond the vertical point towards the opposite bank of the river, then the fish is pulled to land by means of the aforesaid rope or lyams so that there is little chance of him escaping in his struggles for freedom.

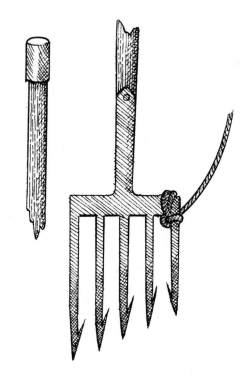

A LEISTERING EXPEDITION

This was organised salmon poaching on a grand scale where blazing pine torches or cressets were used by a team of wild Highlanders wielding leisters in the flickering light.

'All being ready a light was struck and the spark being applied to rags steeped in pitch and fragments of tar barrels, they blazed up at once amid the gloom like the sudden flash from the crater of a volcano. The ruddy light glared on the rough features and dark dresses of the leisterers in cutting flames directly met by black shadows. It reddened the shelving rocks above and glanced upon the blasted arms of the trees slowly perishing in their struggle for existence amongst the stony crevices: it glowed upon the hanging wood, on fir, birch, broom and bracken, half veiled or half revealed as they were more or less prominent.

The principals now sprang into the boats. Two men regulated the course of the craft with their leisters, the auxiliaries were stationed between them and the light was in the centre of the boat side. As the rude forms of the men rose up in their dark attire, wielding their long leisters with the streaks of light that glared partially upon them, and surrounded as they were by the shades of night, you might almost have fancied yourself in the realms below with Pluto and his grim associates embarked on the Stygian lake.

'Now my lads,' says the master; 'Take your places. Tom stand you next to me; Sandy go on the other side of Tom and do you, Jamie, keep in the middle and take tent to cap the boats well over the rapids. Rob, do you and Tom Purdie keep good lights and fell the fish.'

The Snatching Hook

The hook is four or five inches in length. It has a shank which is hollow. The point may be barbed or it may not. In the shank there is a hole through which a strong rope is tied and the strands of the rope are bound down neatly. The rope may be five or six feet long and at its end is a loop through which a man could put his hand. The gaff is not a gaff until the poacher cuts himself a stick. As a rule the stick could be mistaken for a walking stick, a hazel rod such as any idling countryman might have in his hand when walking by the river.

A fine salmon lashes its tail and throws itself at the torrent. The leap fails and it drifts back. The man among the small stones and shingle plays with his stick. The salmon tries again and again. Now it floats back exhausted and lies in a near-at-hand pool recovering its strength, silvered and magnificent, a thing to take the breath away.

The man by the water fumbles in his pocket, draws out the hook, drives his stick into the socket, pulls the rope tight so that all is firm and looks round. In that instant he makes up his mind. The cold mountain water may swirl round his boots but he will not feel its icy bite. The rod and the hook reach out suddenly and the salmon will thresh the water as it slashes into its side. For perhaps three minutes the tug-of-war will go on. The hazel rod no longer needed will swim dizzily round the next pool and then come among the rocks. The salmon, hauled to the side and cracked on the head will cease to struggle, and the poacher will scramble to the nearest cover to hide it or pop it into a sack.

Bream Poachers

In those hard times any fish, flesh or fowl could be used in the kitchen, even gulls and shelduck which they made into sausages. Coarse fish not usually eaten today were a marketable commodity in 1910 in rural Norfolk. Here one Adam Bede was on the run, or rather on the sail, in escape from the pursuing police.

He came sailing downstream with two others aboard the wherry 'plimsol down' with the weight of great whopping bream. Three policemen were pursuing the craft alongshore on bikes. Through the Vauxhall bridge the poaching craft glided, the constables having to make a detour to the Bowling Green pub where they expected the wherry would draw up. But Adam was not going that way, you bet.

As they touched the corner of the Knowl, up went sail and they took fair wind to Breydon, and while one tended the tiller and sail, the others weighted the nets and dropped them into the water, as they thought, opposite a certain numbered post or stake, but the tide took it aslant as it sank and they never afterwards recovered it. The fish were thrown overboard too, many to sink, but others with distended bladders floated down to the sea on the ebb. But for this mishap, the trio got off free.

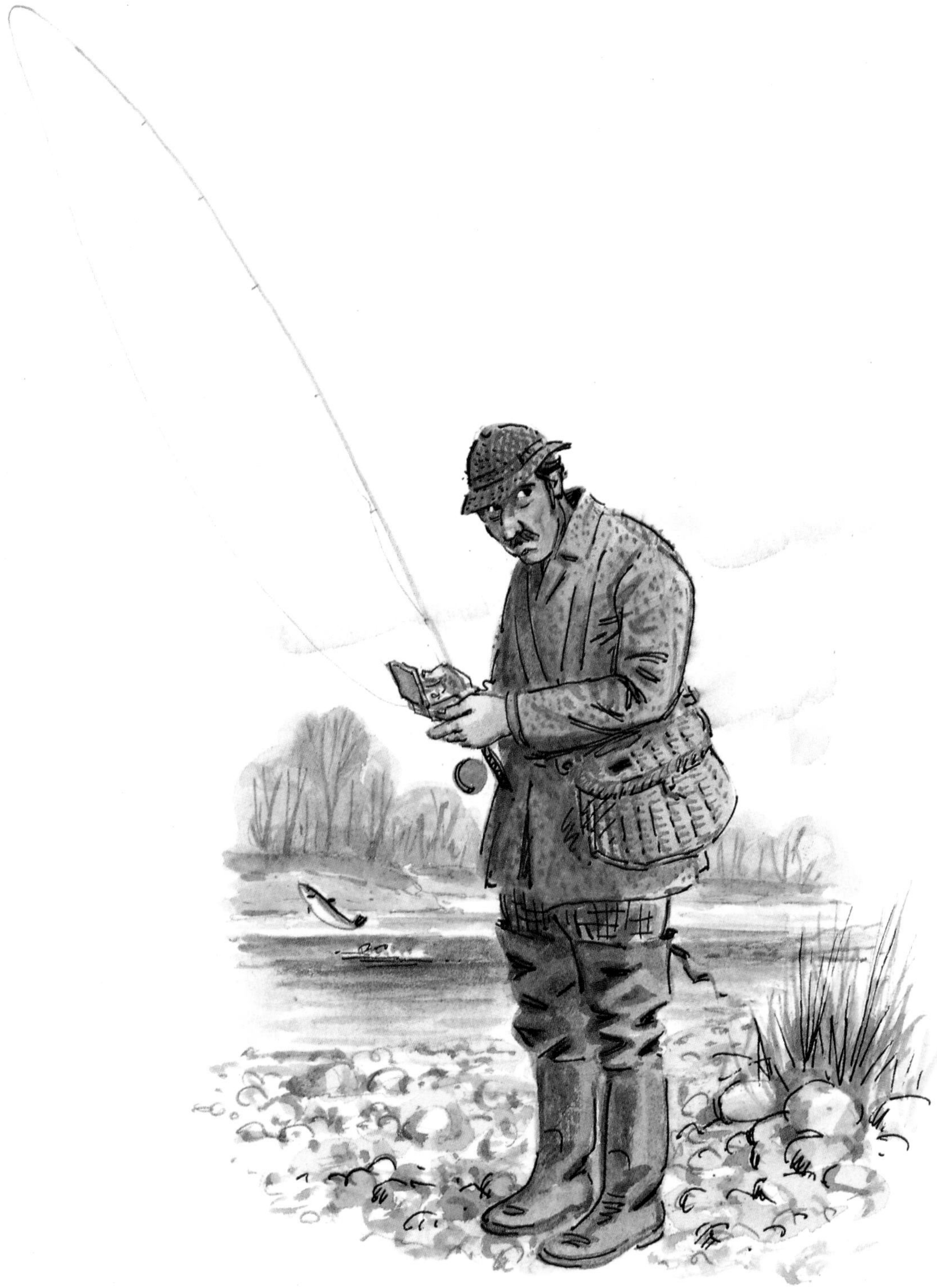

From Wild Sports of the Highlands *by Charles St John*

CHARLES ST JOHN'S HIGHLAND POACHER

The life of a Highland poacher is a far different one from that of an Englishman following the same profession. Instead of a sneaking, night-walking ruffian, a mixture of cowardice and ferocity, as most English poachers are, and ready to commit any crime which he hopes to perpetrate with impunity, the Highlander is a bold, fearless fellow, shooting openly by daylight, taking his sport in the same manner as the laird or the Sassenach who rents the ground.

THE BADENOCH LEISTERERS

Every now and then a salmon would be seen hoisted in the air and quivering on an uplifted spear. The fish as soon as it was caught was carried ashore where it was knocked on the head and taken charge of by some man older than the rest who was deputed to this office. Thirty-seven salmon were killed that night, and I must say that I entered into the fun unmindful of its not being quite in accordance with my ideas of right and wrong and I probably enjoyed it quite as much as any of the wild lads that were engaged in it. There was not much English spoken in the party as they found more expressive words in Gaelic to vent their eagerness and impatience.

What with the sale of these different kinds of game and a tolerable sum made by breaking dogs, a number of young men in the Highlands make a very good income during the shooting season which enables them to live in idleness the rest of the year and often affords them the means of emigrating to America where they settle quietly down and become extensive and steady farmers.

SMALL BEAST IN HODDEN GREY

The rabbit is 'the meek who has inherited the earth', proof against the worst Man can do to it, including germ warfare, shot, trap, snare, net, ferret and dog. I swear that on the day after the last holocaust a pair of grey ears will rise cautiously above the smoking ashes of our world.

Imported by the Normans for its fur, the humble rabbit has kept alive many a yeoman and peasant family in the quiet villages up and down old Britain. Used as presents from squire to peasantry at Christmas, tips by keepers, the fur used to trim copious bonnets, farmed commercially, and exploited as target practice for fledgeling shooters since the days of the crossbow, the rabbit is an integral thread in the tapestry of rural and sporting life in these islands. Our history would have been different without it.

For the poacher it was tasty, catchable, common, untraceable, valuable, barterable and renewable; of what game species could one ask more?

FERRETING

Traditionally the casual poacher ferrets, and in the days when the rabbit was a valuable commodity a couple of lads with ferrets could be a nuisance. For poaching purposes they would use old ferrets with no teeth or young ones with teeth broken. This prevented a kill underground and consequent 'lay-up', for poachers could hardly afford to dig, but wanted to be in and out as quickly as possible. If someone approached whilst they were at their work, they had but to lie flat on the ground and thus would escape detection, unless the keeper actually trod on them.

RICHARD JEFFERIES ON OLD TRICKS

THE SPRINGE

A stout switch was thrust into the ground and bent over in an arch. When the wire was thrown it instantly released the springe which sprung up and drew it fast round the neck of the hare or rabbit whose fore feet were lifted from the earth. Sometimes a growing sapling was bent down for the bow if it chanced to stand conveniently near a run. The hare no sooner put her head in the noose than she was suspended and strangled.

I tried the springe several times for rabbits, and found it answer, but the poacher cannot use it because it is too conspicuous. The stick itself rising above the grass, is visible at some distance and when thrown, it holds the hare or rabbit up for anyone to see who passes by. With a wire set in the present manner the captured animal lies extended and often rolls into a furrow and is further hidden.

Springes with horsehair nooses on the ground were also set for woodcock and wild duck. It is said that a springe of somewhat similar construction was used for pheasants. Horsehair nooses are still applied for capturing woodpeckers and the owls that spend their day in hollow trees, being set round the hole by which they leave the tree. A more delicate horsehair noose is sometimes set for finches and small birds. I tried it for bulfinches, but did not succeed from lack of the dexterity required.

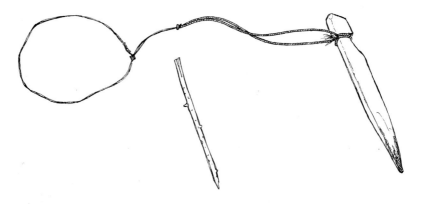

SULPHER

Sulpher fumes were used in attempting to make rabbits bolt from their buries when there was no ferret. I tried an experiment in a bury once with a mixture, the chief component of which was gunpowder, so managed as to burn slowly and give a great smoke. The rabbits did, indeed, just hop out but they hopped in again; and it is a most clumsy expedient, because the fire must be lit on the windward side, and the rabbits will only come out to leeward. The smoke hangs and does not penetrate into half the tunnels, or else it blows through quickly when you must stop half the holes with a spade. It is a wretched substitute for a ferret.

THE GIN

Alfred Curtis explains how he used to set up a gin trap to catch rabbits.

In the Spring when the buck rabbits were full of the urge to breed, I would catch a doe and skin it, scrape up the loose earth from the little latrines that rabbits scoop out for themselves and rub the earth round the inside of the skin. Then I covered my gin trap with that earth and I knew I should catch a buck.

Out he would come, sniff, sniff, hopping big-eyed with desire – the sniff, sniff again at the scent of the doe and stamp, stamp his little forepaws would go, and ping! he was prisoner.

'LITTLE JOHN' KILLS A RABBIT

From The Amateur Poacher *by Richard Jefferies.*

There was a low rumbling sound – I expected to see a rabbit bolt into one of my nets. I heard Little John moving some leaves and then he shouted, 'Give I a net, you – quick! Lor! here be another hole: he's coming!' I looked over the mound and saw Little John, his teeth set and staring at a hole which had no net, his great hands open ready to pounce instantly like some wild animal on its prey. In an instant the rabbit bolted – he clutched it and clasped it tight to his chest. There was a moment of struggling, the next the rabbit was held up for a moment and then cast across his knee.

It was always a sight to see Little John's keen delight in 'wristing' their necks. He affected utter unconsciousness of what he was doing, looked you in the face, and spoke of some indifferent subject. But all the while he was feeling the rabbit's muscles stretch before the terrible grasp of his hands, and an expression of complacent satisfaction flitted over his features as the neck gave with a sudden looseness, and in a moment what had been a living, straining creature, became limp.

A Dangerous Rabbit

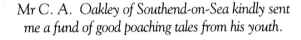

Mr C. A. Oakley of Southend-on-Sea kindly sent me a fund of good poaching tales from his youth.

One evening Ed was out to get a couple of rabbits from a burrow on the estate close to his tin hut home. He took a friend, whom we shall call Sid, as a lookout. On this occasion he decided to use ferrets. Posting Sid nearby, he set about netting the hole and put down the ferret.

Ten minutes passed and he peered down the hole, and saw a rabbit trapped between the exit and the ferret, so he put down his arm to grab it. Being rather on the short side he could not quite reach it, so he called Sid who was much longer in the arm and asked him to have a go. Sid bent down to have a look, and as he got down to eye level the ferret moved and the rabbit bolted, coming out of the hole like a rocket and striking Sid fair and square between the eyes.

The force of the blow threw him backwards and knocked him unconscious. Ed was convulsed with laughter – as were the two keepers, who were spying on them from nearby. They came up, rendered first aid, and promptly pinched the two of them for poaching. All was done with great good humour.

CADGER'S RABBIT

Arthur Patterson wrote about the strange characters, fowlers, poachers and 'Sons of Ishmael' who haunted Breydon Water at the turn of the century. His book Wildfowlers and Poachers *is a collectable classic. Cadger was suspected of having stolen a very large, black-and-white rabbit, an instantly recognisable animal. The local detective had been sent to await the arrival of Cadger's wherry in the hope of finding evidence.*

... in due course it arrived at the Brick Quay and was brought up, a rope being thrown ashore which Lingwood [the detective] obligingly fastened to a mooring stump.

'You've got a lovely smell leaking from that cabin,' remarked the detective. 'I'd say you've got something on the way that smells just lovely – smells wonderfully like stewed rabbit.'

'Rabbit it is, my boy,' admitted Cadger, 'and it's a beauty. Why not step aboard and try a leg!' 'You do live well, what with hares an' coots an' plovers an' long-tails!' said Lingwood, holding his plate for another helping of rabbit, onion and potato. 'A fine rabbit, too, and what a lovely skin he must hev worn. Can yer let me hev it?'

'Whatever for?' asked Cadger, opening wide his eyes. 'Why, to hev it cured; what a lovely, warm chest protector it would make.' 'There now,' said the poacher, 'if I'd only know'd you wanted it I'd a' seft it for yer. What a pity.' 'Well, what the dooce hev ye done with it?' demanded the detective with a changed expression on his face. 'Well, bor Lingwood: it's like this here; when I hev a rabbit for dinner, *I allus eats the skin fust!*'

As a matter of fact, Cadger had gone into the cabin immediately on jumping aboard the wherry as she was leaving the dyke and carefully skinned the rabbit, and then having tied one of the bricks from the cargo to the skin, quietly dropped it overboard. No-one used the word 'rabbit' again in Lingwood's hearing once the story leaked out.

POOR MAN'S LONG NET

A crafty and easy way of catching a few rabbits with minimum fuss, little risk and no skill was for a few lads to wait on a light night until the rabbits were far out on a field feeding. Locating their holes in the fence bottom – the lads would have done their homework by daylight so they knew roughly where to look – they would cram a close-fitting lump of turf to an arm's length inside each hole. The outlying rabbits were then beaten in; they would dash into what they believed to be the safety of their holes, but found they could get no further than a little way in. It was then an easy matter for the poacher to push in his arm and drag them out.

LONGTAILS

The pheasant – a foolish, strutting bird, popular with the well-to-do who value its sporting powers and strong flight, epitome of gourmet fare on the table, imported from China by the Romans who knew a good thing when they saw it – has been responsible for more expenditure, sorrow, injury and death than any other bird in the kingdom.

The sportsman who fills his woods with pheasants and sets a man to protect them is an object of interest to the poacher who likes a spot of pheasant on his plate and knows of others who would gladly buy such a bird from him, so over the years he has devised ways many and artful to come to terms with it. He risked transportation or shooting or prison, and would fight like a tiger to avoid such fates, but surely such a noble bird was well worth the sacrifice.

THE LONE SHOOTER

Perhaps the hardest of all to deal with was, and is, the poacher who shoots at night on his own. Such a one can prove an expensive adversary, unless dropped on by pure good luck as he rounds a bend and walks into the arms of the keeper. His tactic is to shoot and move, never staying in one spot long enough for the watchers to pinpoint him and come to the place. He enters the coverts at night and, keeping near a path, makes a note of every roosting pheasant as he goes. When farthest from home he retraces his steps taking the birds he has marked earlier, avoiding those near tangled undergrowth, shooting and running to the next place until, with as many as he can carry, he leaves the wood at the point he entered it.

The keeper hears the first shot and rushes to the place, but too late; there is no-one there. Then he hears another and again runs forward, then a third shot rings out, until in the end the firing ceases and he has lost his man. The best advice for a keeper is to lie in wait at a spot nearest the wood exit, for there is a chance that the poacher will come home by that route. At least by staying in one place he has more chance of an arrest than by blundering about chasing will o' the wisps. Sometimes such a poacher would lie low for a good half-hour waiting for the coast to clear. A waiting keeper should be equally patient and not give up his vigil until certain that the intruder has gone.

SNARING AT ROOST

In coverts where the trees are not of any great height, some poachers will snare roosting pheasants with a wire slip-noose on the end of a pole. This is best done with young and foolish pheasants in October in the days before they have learned sense; though even then it is a very uncertain game.

The pole is constructed along the lines of a fishing rod so that its length can easily be increased or diminished to suit the height of the tree. The noose is fastened to the end, the other end of the string running down to the hands of the poacher. A young pheasant is not easily disturbed when it has gone up to roost and the poacher is helped by the bird's instinct to poke out its neck to see better

what the commotion below is about. Assuming that there are not too many twigs in the way and all things being favourable, the poacher may slip his noose round the neck of the bird and snatch it down to him. This is a silent method and therefore hard to detect and while a poacher will have many failures, the man who wants only a bird or two for himself will find the method a good one.

The only signs that snaring has been carried out are sprays of feathers and dislodged earth on the ground for the bird flails its wings mightily as it is being drawn down. Some poachers use a spring-clip instead of a noose which grasps the bird and holds it securely.

WOODEN PHEASANTS

A common dodge was for the keeper to carve a number of pheasants from wood, inserting the tail feathers of a real bird to aid realism. These he would set on likely branches near paths and rides, though not where members of the public could see them. The poacher would see one silhouetted against the night sky and fire a shot. He might be surprised that the bird did not fall, but not that it did not fly away, for roosting pheasants can take a great deal of disturbing. He takes careful aim and fires his second shot, but with the same effect.

With luck he would go from dummy to dummy, growing more puzzled by the minute. Many such wooden pheasants were found to be plastered with shot fired at them by unsuspecting poachers. The wise keeper would move the birds from time to time as pheasants do not roost every night on the same twig, and the poacher would grow suspicious unless their locations were regularly shifted.

Cruder models have also proved successful: chicken wire roughly shaped and covered with sacking, tin cutouts, straw 'dolly' pheasants, and even whole sugar-beet with a crudely fashioned head attached – all had their day and doubtless saved many a real bird from premature death. In each case the model would have the tail feathers of a real pheasant inserted.

A good idea once is a good idea always, and this very day I see the 'Pheasifoil' has hit the market place. This is our old friend the model pheasant designed to be fixed in a tree to fool poachers. There is little new under the sun. The Pheasifoil makes use of modern technology, for it contains an inflated balloon and when this is punctured by a shot or a stone from a catapult and the air released a trigger is activated and a 100-decibel alarm sounds, more than enough the wake the dead and certainly to bring a sleepy keeper from his bed and provide the poacher with a shock from which it will take him some days to recover.

Made of a synthetic material and machine-produced, this is a most realistic bird, especially when painted in pheasant colours, though the addition of real pheasant tail feathers is recommended, even to this hi-tec device.

FIRE AND BRIMSTONE

A popular myth and one of the oldest of old wives' tales concerns the legendary method of stupefying a roosting pheasant with the fumes from a blend of oily rags and sulpher; these put in an old tin, lighted, and puffed until they smoked mightily. The smoke was to be conducted by means of a long pipe up to the head of the pheasant roosting above until, overcome by the fumes, it came crashing down.

We have tried this method ourselves (strictly in the line of research) with palpable lack of success, and no-one can be found who admits to having tried it successfully. Until such a person may be found, this wonderful theory must continue to be regarded as a fabulous myth.

WOOD BLINDNESS

Alfred Curtis worked hard to feed his family.

For minutes on end, for half an hour, an hour, I peered into the lacing of the boughs, seeing nothing but the grey of the sky behind and the interweaving branches and blobs that were pheasants. I made the cross on the tree, seeing it still interlaced with the tracery of boughs. I went to the next tree and peering up saw the same boughs I had seen before and before that and all evening. I was blind with wood blindness known only to poachers and keepers.

I crouched where I was, there on the earth and buried head in hands waiting for sight to return and Bill waited beside me, gun resting lightly in his arm, ears alert for the first warning sound. At last the blindness passed away and the trees came back to their own form. There we might rest until day was near for the pheasants would wait..

MARKING THE TREES

We needed only a .410 gun, a pocketful of cartridges and a lump of whitening, the sort that was used by everybody to whiten the hearth, a penny a lump. We peered into the boughs till we made out the dark blob of a pheasant and then on that tree we made a large cross with our whitening, facing so that we should see it on our return.

ONE FOR THE POT

There were many ways by which a man could by ingenuity take a few birds for himself and stand a good chance of escaping detection. Grain soaked in brandy was a favourite; the birds became stupefied by the liquor and could be picked up before they recovered. Raisins on fish hooks were also worth a try, but these were best used on a springing bough so that the bird could not get a direct pull on the line and break it.

Trailing the birds away by feeding them was harder to bring about. Favourite foods like black oats and buckwheat which were hard to see on the ground, and old favourites such as raisins or acorns, could be used to lead the birds from home. Much value was placed in the dari seed which is said to be a special favourite, drawing birds great distances. On one farm it was thought that every covey of partridges on the place had gathered on the one field where dari seed had been spread.

On one occasion a keeper stood idly watching the shepherd busying himself round his sheep-fold. He noticed that the man had a bag of corn on his back; nothing odd in that, until he noticed the shepherd set off in the direction of the nearest covert which was a hundred yards or so away. Looking round to make sure he was not observed the shepherd pulled a plug of straw from the bottom of his bag and walked slowly back, allowing a trickle of corn to leak from the bag onto the ground behind him. Thus he returned to the sheep-fold.

The keeper was about to rush out in indignation and accuse the man, but then reflected that proof was hard to supply and the man would certainly deny that he had done any wrong. He waited, watched and bided his time until one morning he found a pheasant in a snare in the sheep-fold. The shepherd's task was made easier because pheasants often frequent places where there are animals, going there for spilled food; so the shepherd had little trouble in attracting the odd bird to his traps.

From The Amateur Poacher *by Richard Jefferies.*

COCK FIGHTING

When cock fighting was common, the bellicose inclinations of the cock pheasant were sometimes excited even to its own destruction. A game cock was first armed with the sharp spur made of the best razors and then put down near where a cock pheasant had been observed to crow. The pheasant cock is thoroughly game, and will not allow any rival crowing in his locality; the two therefore quickly met in battle. Like a keen poniard, the game-cock's spur either slew the pheasant outright or got fixed in the pheasant's feathers when he was captured.

VARIOUS TRICKS

The partridges were sometimes driven into the nets by a dog. The partridges that appear on the first of September are said to be netted, though probably by those who have a right to do so. These birds by nature lend themselves to such tricks, being so timid. It is said that if continually driven to and fro they will, at the last, just cower in one spot, and can be taken by hand or knocked over with a stick.

The sight of a paper kite in the air makes them motionless till forced to rise; and there was an old dodge of ringing a bell at night, which so alarmed the covey that they remained still till the net was ready, when a sudden flash of light drove them into it. Imagine a poacher ringing a bell nowadays! The partridges then were peculiarly liable to be taken; now, perhaps, they escape better than any other kind of game. Except with a gun the poacher can hardly touch them, and after the coveys have broken up it is not worth his while to risk a shot very often. If only their eggs could be protected there should be little difficulty in maintaining partridge numbers.

SNARING PHEASANTS

This was a far more successful and often-used system, and it operated in much the same way as snaring rabbits. Pheasants always prefer to run rather than fly, and this habit makes them vulnerable to the snarer. His ideal site would be a narrow belt of trees or scrub connecting one wood with another, and half-way down this he would make a secure little fence of small bushes and various brash collected from round about. This fence would be stout, but not easily noticed by a passing keeper; a good man could make such a fence and it would escape detection for a season, even though the keeper might be often in the wood.

At every yard interval the poacher would leave a gap large enough for a pheasant to run through, and across it would bend a bowed stick with each end stuck in the ground, and would hang a snare made of a single strand of wire from the exact centre of each one. Making his way back to the end of the wood the poacher would beat the covert, walking in a zig-zag manner and covering all the ground, driving the running birds before him. If caught in the act he is an innocent man out for a few blackberries or to cut a stick – search him and there is nothing incriminating on his person.

When the pheasants arrive at the newly made fence they head straight for the openings, their heads are caught in the nooses and they are soon choked by their struggles. The poacher comes up, removes the birds, goes to the other end of the belt and repeats the process. The fence may be left in place for a future visit when a few cunning repairs will quickly have it back in service.

This is a deadly method which accounted for a great many birds.

INSTANT HEDGE FOR PHEASANTS

Alfred Curtis has a successful night.

As I cut and the pile of little stakes grew, he set to work on the hedge, criss-crossing the twigs, putting back the grasses and vegetation so that nothing showed, and so he worked his way twenty yards or so through the wood. Every two or three feet where a branch hung conveniently overhead Lammie left a gap big enough for a pheasant to go through.

We went along the fence and in each gap Lammie place some food, pheasant food, a few raisins, a sprinkle of corn and some blackberries. There was more food each side of the gap so that from whichever way the pheasant came there was something to lead him into the gap and through. We passed another night in the woods and in the morning the food had all gone. Again we fed the gaps and it was the third day. Lammie said, 'Alf, you get some more blackberries and the last of the food; I'm going to feed again tonight and the next night we shall take the lot.'

At every gap a branch hung down held lightly under a notch on another twig pushed into the ground and to each branch was tied a wire noose and every noose was held by a twig ready for a pheasant to run into.

We awoke at first light but did not go straight to our fence. We went to the outside of the wood and took a good look around then worked back through the wood from opposite ends, zig zagging and making plenty of noise and a fine time we had of it after all those hours of enforced silence.

When we came to our fence there were pheasants red and gold above our heads and among them a rabbit or two still limp and warm. We set to cutting them down and destroyed the fence, hiding the sticks in thickets and throwing the rest in the stream.

We washed in the stream, our first wash for days, made ourselves presentable and went home with empty hands. There we shaved and put on what good clothes we might have and set forth again each carrying a carpet bag for tools with a tool or two showing for all to see. Back at the haystack we filled those bags with all they could carry and set off home again like respectable artisans with not a breath of suspicion about us.

I went with Lammie again after to different woods and many a pheasant has walked home in that carpet bag and so to the tables of those who know good food when they see it.

A Ploughboy's Trick

James Wentworth Day was one of the great writers about field sports, the Fenlands and the countryside generally. In his fine book Sporting Adventure, *he explains ingenious ways of taking pheasants.*

I think I prefer the ploughboy trick we had of making a dozen cones of thick brown paper, like ice cream cones, smearing the insides with bird lime, filling the bottoms with maize and then sticking them in the newly ploughed furrows just outside the covertside.

The pheasants were bound to come sneaking out for worms and grubs and equally bound to stick their beaks into the cones. And then the cones stuck and half a dozen old cocks and hens would be tumbling wildly about with April Fool's caps stuck over their eyes, too blinded and too bewildered to fly.

You can, of course, take your pheasants by salting their feeding grounds with maize soaked in gin – they provide a perfect 'morning after' police court parade – or choke them with peas through which are threaded horse hairs, but that is a cad's trick.

The crude method of shooting them at roost is not to be recommended. In the first place, if the keeper has a sense of humour he will plaster the trees nearest the rides with wooden dummies. In the second place, the orthodox method of carrying a short barrelled gun down the leg of one's trousers and trying to look like a wooden legged sailor has its drawbacks. I know a man who tried it. The gun went off. He has a wooden leg now.

Dropped a Brace
....

Gil Gaylor, the Gatcombe Park poacher recalls a lucky escape.

I had not time to collect my thoughts as I pelted across the fields to reach the stream. The immediate necessity was to put enough distance between me and the young gamekeeper and his dogs. Eventually I slowed down and with the sleeping fields all around me I sat down in a dry ditch under a hedge feeling breathless.

I was a good two miles from forbidden territory and I reflected on the night's events. I thought with some satisfaction of the young keeper and how I had managed to fool him yet again – by my jumping the stream his dogs would lose the scent. Luckily they had barked when some way off and this had given me time to make my escape. Half-an-hour before I had shot three brace of pheasants with the catapult.

Then it was that suddenly I realised that somewhere in my flight I had dropped a brace, and I cursed my carelessness. The keeper would surely find the birds on the rideway, examine them and find they had been shot with a catapult. Knowing me and my reputation his thoughts would turn my way and he would nail the crime to me. But I chuckled to myself as I sat smoking a roll-up. I had evaded capture yet again.

OWEN THE WHIP

Ian Niall tells of an unusual pheasant-catching technique!

Owen poached only once in his life by the strangest method one is likely ever to hear. He drove a van for a country butcher in the days before motor vans buzzed round the farms and villages. He was sitting up behind his horse, letting the tired creature take its time on a long hill when he saw before him three pheasants feeding on a bank above the road. There was plenty of time to think. Owen looked for a weapon. There were no loose stones by the roadside, he had no hidden gun, but his eye caught his whip.

At a distance of a few yards from the feeding birds he drew up the horse and stepped quietly down onto the grass verge. Somehow the movement of the horse or even a man on foot on a road does not excite a feeding bird or animal. Owen crawled up the bank without a sound. The hen pheasant nearest him jerked up her head in alarm and in that instant the whip cracked out and coiled itself about her neck and she scrambled and fluttered on the grass. The cock and the other hens burst into flight as Owen threw himself on top of the bank and grabbed the hen before she could become disentangled and take flight. The practised hand of the butcher's man quickly wrung her neck and, when the horse began its journey again and Owen leant forward on his seat to replace his whip, the pheasant lay behind him under the canvas.

DUBIOUS EVIDENCE

The late Richard (Dick) Walker was internationally acclaimed as a famous angler, long-standing record-holder for the best common carp, writer of some classic fishing books and trail-blazer for many of the angling styles now in common usage. His widow Pat Walker has kindly sent me Dick's own account of a poaching exploit carried out by him in times of wartime shortages.

Some of my colleagues and I did succeed in supplementing our rations by shooting a variety of wildlife, including grey squirrels, rabbits, hares and pheasants. On one occasion my driver Vic Page and I stopped twice on our way through Norfolk to Bircham Newton. We were equipped with a .45 revolver for which Page had a proper firearms certificate, and a .22 Remington rifle with a telescopic sight – with which I shot two pheasants.

After shooting the second one we had gone no further than a couple of hundred yards, when out of the ditch covered with camouflage vines sprang one PC George Mortar, who stopped us and said, 'You will be charged with killing game,' and so on. Having examined our two pheasants he said, (and I quote) 'Gor bugger boy, you don't miss much, do you?'

He asked to search the van, but we pointed the Webley revolver at him and said 'No, you mustn't, it's filled with secret equipment' – which was true! He had the good sense not to press the point, but he did report us and we were charged with killing game without a licence. In due course we appeared at the Magistrates' Court at the Petty Sessional Division of Smithton and Brothercross in the county of Norfolk; we pleaded guilty.

The constable gave evidence in the most formal 'out-of-the-notebook' way. The Chairman of the Magistrates asked 'Have you anything to say?' to which I replied 'No, Sir, except the evidence that the constable gave was not quite exact.' The Chairman said 'In what respect was it incorrect?,' and I replied 'Well, he didn't say: "I have reason to believe that you have just shot a pheasant." What he *did* say was "Gor bugger boy, you don't miss much, do you?"' There followed what the press usually describe as 'laughter in court', which went on for a long time and involved the entire bench of Magistrates as well as members of the public and press. Then the Chairman said 'Constable Mortar, is what the Defendant says true?' The constable stood up and said 'Yes, Sir' and sat down again. The Chairman conferred with his colleagues and said 'You will be fined £1 each – that is our usual price for pheasant-poaching – and you will remain at the back of the court until the Court rises.'

When the Court rose this gentleman, who was a retired Colonel, strode up to us and said 'Now, you young devils, if you want to shoot my pheasants in future do me the courtesy of asking my permission first, and you may come and shoot two or three whenever you want.' We became friends with him, and never abused his hospitality; we never shot more than we were allowed, and it did supplement our meagre meat ration for the rest of the war.

It was an interesting episode, and I have laughed about it ever since. It is the only time I ever got caught poaching, and I should have been more careful! It's not as if I haven't done much poaching: I am not ashamed to admit that from school-days, through university and right through the war, I did plenty. It transpired that we fell into a trap laid by the Norfolk police to catch some Canadians who had been shooting at anything that moved with everything that they had, including Sten guns and even Very pistols. It was them, and not us, that the police were trying to catch!

WILKINS' WOODEN PHEASANTS

John Wilkins used wooden pheasants with great success.

Monk and his two comrades shot six times at my false wooden pheasants which I used to nail up in the trees in place where poachers would be likely to see them. They fired three double shots at one bird and then climbed up the tree to see if old Satan was there, for they had shot it full in the breast, then in the right side and then in the left and still the bird kept sitting serenely on. Then they gave in, having fired off six barrels and getting nothing for their pains but loss of time and waste of powder and shot. Monk got something, however, in the shape of six months in Chelmsford gaol.

PUSS
IN THE CORN

The hare was large, of predictable habits, good to eat and catchable by a man who knew his business. It was also a creature of mystery and romance, linked in ancient mythology with the moon, the seasons, with madness and dim, pagan memories. It slept, they said, with its eyes open, always ran away uphill and seemed to abandon its young in the middle of open fields.

It also ran through well-worn runs in hedges or slipped under gates. A fast dog could take one, while its habit of sitting in a form pretending to be invisible made it vulnerable to a moucher who had seen it before it saw him. A wise poacher stuck to hares and rabbits – less fuss and easier all round – and left the pheasants alone, but a keeper finding snares would keep watch and was not averse, let it be whispered, to 'planting' the evidence of a dead hare in the noose. 'Puss' was at the bottom of much rural grief in the post Game Laws era.

HARES

'As I was a'reaping near famed Wantage town,
A gurt hare came leaping so sleek and so brown,
But me being gifted like David with sling,
A smooth stone I lifted and dropped her at spring.'

PATRICK CHALMERS

The poacher's favourite time to attack hares was in the spring when the animals began to graze the fields of young clover; hares dearly love a clover field, as they do an oat stubble, and next to that a field of tender young corn. In the spring the hares would be mating and conspicuous with their wooing, chasing here and there, boxing each other with a blur of paws, and making their presence felt to eyes far less keen than those of the moucher lurking near the gateway. Also, it was a widely accepted belief that hares could not resist parsley, and when the farmer drilled his clover some poachers would go so far as to throw in a few handfuls of parsley seed; conversely, those who kept hares in captivity and studied them held the view that money spent thus was money wasted, and that hares preferred clover to parsley any time.

A hare does not graze as methodically as a rabbit but nibbles a plant here and a plant there, where its small cousin would systematically strip a limited area. Hares grazing young corn always provided a source of friction between keeper and farmer – the latter would go to the keeper and complain bitterly about hare damage and the fact that he had seen no less than eleven of the monsters on his nine-acre that very morning. The traditional response had to do, namely that for each blade bitten off two would grow in its place so that in fact the hares were doing the farmer a favour.

There was an element of truth in this, for unless it was eaten down again and again, an early graze of young cereals always seemed to strengthen the crop rather than weaken it.

GATE-NETTING

The poachers would have plenty of opportunity to see where the hares were feeding and playing, and they would return under cover of darkness armed with a loose square of netting of 3in mesh just the height and width of an ordinary field gate. It would be loosely hitched to each gate post, the top edge weighted down on the upper rail with a line of small stones.

Hares will often make for gateways when started and seem to know their exact whereabouts. The poachers would choose a windy night, with the wind blowing the scent of the netter away from the quarry; one man would then hide near the net, and the other drive the field with the aid of a lurcher dog. The hare would race for the gate, straight into the net which it would pull down upon itself, and the man in ambush would nip out and put an end to its struggles.

The only way the keeper could prevent gate-netting was to stop the hares using the gates as field exits. Most effective was to nail an extra rung or two on the bottom of the gate so that the hares could not possibly squeeze through; sometimes he would simply lower the bottom rail, with the same result. Rather less certain was the practice recommended by some, of the keeper himself gate-netting the hares and releasing them a few times, thus teaching the hares to give gates a wide berth.

SNARING HARES

On those fields where a vigilant keeper has used some dodge to prevent gate-netting, a poacher might line an entire hedge or fence with snares and drive the hares into them. This is a mob-handed job, requiring a considerable gang. A long fence or hedge on one side of a field or fields – maybe half a mile long – is snared, a bright moonlit night being chosen the better for the poachers to see what they are doing.

Waiting a while to allow the human taint to evaporate from the snares and pegs, they would go off and drive the fields towards them. The shriek of a snared hare once heard is not easily forgotten – it is very piercing, and any waiting keeper would hear it at some distance. Signs of a struggle round the site of the snare will show where a hare has been taken, and – as with the long-netter and his hazel pegs – it is rare that a gang would pick up every single snare in its haste to escape, so the keeper has a clear indication as to what has taken place.

Far more deadly is the single poaching labourer who sets a few snares for himself when he thinks no-one is about. The keeper happening to find such a snare should examine it carefully to see if it is new. An odd snare left by a gang is not likely to be of any interest for they will hardly return for one, but a fresh snare is worth watching. The keeper should consider carefully the possible routes the poacher might have used to approach, and lie in ambush.

A Rick-top Vigil

A certain keeper found just such a snare set in the hedge, and there happening to be a convenient straw-stack nearby, he made himself a snug nest in a hole near the top and hid in it to await the return of the poacher; by popping up his head now and then he could keep a clear watch on the two paths which passed the spot. Unfortunately, he chose to pop up his head just as the poacher was making a stealthy and unseen approach from behind his position.

The poacher, being possessed of a mischievous sense of humour, sauntered by in a deliberately suspicious manner, doing everything possible to arouse the excitement of the watcher, but without actually touching or looking at the snare. He kept this up for the whole day and only abandoned the ruse at nightfall, thereby keeping the keeper in a state of constant suspense but with nothing to show for his patience.

Another watcher hid in a brick sheep-fold in sight of a snare set in a gateway. A labourer passed by and happened to see him peeping out. The man was a companion of poachers and a few yards down the road he met the owner of the snare and advised him, in full hearing of the watcher: 'Don't go near that sheep-pen, mate; farmer Barnes has shut a bear in it!'

The watcher could easily be deluded by those poachers and their accomplices confident of their craft. A snare was found with a hare actually in it within a hundred yards of the bailiff's house and the underkeeper was set to keep a close eye on it. The keeper hid behind a fence nearby and settled down to a long wait.

By and by the bailiff wandered by looking round this way and that, and saw the keeper in his hiding-place. Enquiring as to his business the bailiff expressed surprise and indignation that anyone could be so bold as to snare a hare so close to his house. After some conversation the bailiff invited the keeper back to his cottage for a drop of homemade wine. 'It won't sinnify to leave the snare for just a minute.'

The keeper succumbed to temptation and went with this kindly man some liquid refreshment. On his return he was more than annoyed to discover that hare and snare had vanished. 'Who would have thought of them coming when I was away for a moment? They must have been a'watching me.' Indeed they were, for it was the daughter of the bailiff himself who had slipped down the lane and retrieved the booty when the keeper was safely in the kitchen enjoying his drop of grog.

The keeper was wrong to have left his post, but since the bailiff had spotted him he could have waited until Domesday before anyone took the hare. What he might have been better at was guessing the true identity of the culprit. With a little thought he would not have placed himself so close to the bailiff's house, and had he done so he would have made a notable arrest.

It was usual for a poacher to return to his snares early in the morning just as it was making light. The keeper must, therefore, be there before him no matter how foul the weather or hard the early rising. When approaching the place the keeper should be most careful not to let himself be seen but should come by secret paths to the snare.

One keeper knew that a local poacher was in the habit of waiting on the road to shoot hares where they played in the field nearby – at dawn the hares came close to the verge and could easily be shot. The keeper determined on a dawn raid, but on the critical morning he overslept by half an hour and it was broad daylight before he arrived at the place, puffing and panting. Peeping carefully over the hedge he was surprised to see the upturned face of the poacher looking up at him, gun in hand, safe on the highway and also in possession of a licence and therefore technically doing no wrong.

The keeper tried to make the best of it: 'Seen my mate?,' he enquired. 'No, but its lucky I saw you,' chuckled the poacher and tucking his gun under his arm he marched, all innocence, from the scene.

HARES IN ROOTS

When lifting roots such as mangolds, swedes or turnips, some cunning labourers would leave the largest ones standing in the field, sticking up like broken teeth. If the keeper asked about this odd custom, he was told that the master always liked the giant specimens left behind as though by accident, the better to impress other farmers passing by. In fact the labourer knew well that the hares, missing their accustomed glut of food and freedom of choice, would cluster round the few roots which had been purposely left behind; when these appeared to be well gnawed, it was a simple matter to place some gin traps under the rotten leaves and catch a hare.

The arrival of the corn binder and its habit of rattling round the field in ever-decreasing squares was a source of constant anxiety to a keeper. Then, as now, the game animals which love the standing corn for its food and shelter are reluctant to leave the dwindling patch. The harvesters would wait until they were marooned within the last small square, then walk carefully in until they saw a hare or rabbit squatting terrified. It was easy work to bag a number of them with a pitchfork or iron bar.

Harvesters tried to arrange things so they reached that critical point before the end of the day, otherwise the game would creep out under cover of darkness. If they miscalculated and had to leave the last few swathes, they would ring the remaining stand with traps. Alternatively they would return after dark and surround the patch with nets and drive the game out.

Any keeper worth his salt would see to it that he strolled by as the last few cuts were being made, and would run his dogs through the crop as a matter of course. A good keeper was never far from the harvest fields when there was reaping going on.

A PLANTED HARE

From The Amateur Poacher *by Richard Jefferies.*

On the border of a thicket near an open field of swedes we found a hare in a wire. It was a beauty – the soft fur smooth to stroke, not so much as a shot-hole in the black marked ears. Wired or netted hares are much preferred by the dealers to those that have been shot.

To pull up the plug and take the wire and hare too was the first impulse, yet we hesitated. Why did the man who had set the snare allow his game to lie until that hour of the day? It had a suspicious look altogether. Carefully replacing him just as we found him we left the spot and re-entered the copse.

Someone suddenly spoke from behind, and as we turned, there was a man in a velveteen jacket who had just stepped out of the bushes. The keeper was pleasant enough and readily allowed us to handle his gun – a very good weapon, though a little thin at the muzzle – for a man likes to have his gun admired. He said if it was nuts we were after there were finer ones in a valley he pointed out; and then he carefully instructed us how to get back to the waggon track without returning by the same path. An old barn was the landmark, and with a request not to break the bushes, he left us.

Down in the wooded vale we paused. The whole thing was now clear: the hare in the wire was a trap laid for the 'gips' whose camp was below. The keeper had been waiting about doubtless where he could command a good view of the various tracks up the hill, had seen us coming that way and did not wish us to return in the same direction because if the 'gip' saw anyone at all he would not approach his snare. Whether the hare had actually been caught by the wire or had been put in it by the keeper, it was not easy to tell.

THE UNCATCHABLE HARE

Perhaps my favourite Oakley story about Ed concerns the hare too swift for any dog to run down. Ed was left alone after the death of his parents and took to the poaching life, being strictly a 'one for the pot' man, and not commercial. He started out living in a tin shed in Hertfordshire with a lurcher and a .410. This story is set in 1953.

Behind Ed's tin shed was a large field on which lived a very large hare. My dear friend Ed used to watch this hare on many a warm day. He also used to watch many a gypsy and vagabond try his dog against it; lurchers, whippets and even greyhounds were all tried, but they never caught their quarry. They rarely got a second chance before they were chased off the field by the keepers or the village bobby.

One day Ed was supping a well-earned pint in the pub beyond this very cornfield when he overheard two gentlemen in conversation about 'his' hare. 'I'll give five pounds to anybody who's dog can catch that hare,' said one of the gentlemen. Now five pounds was a lot of money in those days, and Ed was in need of something to eat, so he challenged the strangers, claiming that he had the very dog which could catch the hare.

The next day Ed tramped to the nearest car-breaker's yard, a good three miles away. There he purchased on old Austin windscreen which he carried home. An hour before his meeting with the gentlemen he drove the hare to the bottom of the field close to the pub. He then took the windscreen and placed it across the run ten yards from the wood in a spot where the hare could not be seen from the road. Driving two stakes well into the ground the windscreen was stood upright and the glass given a good polish.

He took his dog and returned to the pub for his meeting. He found the two men in the pub with five pounds on the table and a pint in hand, and there they stood waiting for the hare to appear. Ten minutes later it did so and Ed took his dog and the two gentlemen outside. The dog knew his job and on seeing the hare he was released. The hare saw the dog and set off on his usual escape route up the field towards the wood.

The two gentlemen, watching closely, began to snigger, as the dog was making only small progress in reaching the hare. They both disappeared over the brow of the hill with forty yards between them, but only twenty yards to the wood. The men turned, and one of them said, 'I think, my friend, that you owe us five pounds'. Ed, however, said 'No, I think the five pounds in your pocket is mine'. Then he turned and pointed up the field and there, sure enough, was his dog, the hare in its mouth, trotting down the hill.

The men were flabbergasted, and on paying the five pounds left quickly. Not sporting, I know. The hare was just ten yards from freedom when it ran straight into the car windscreen that had been strategically placed across the run. Knocked unconscious, the dog had the chance to catch up and move in for the kill, all this taking place out of sight. Nevertheless, it was one for the pot and a bonus of five pounds in Ed's pocket.

SNARING AND THE VICTORIAN LAW

There is no crime in just looking, and in the eyes of the law the blackest poacher in the village was doing no wrong simply by gazing at a snare. Touching it was a different matter, and a keeper always had to catch his man with his hands on the incriminating evidence if he was to make sure of a conviction. Even then the case was not absolutely safe, for a hare in a snare, especially when visible from the public road, was a temptation to anyone who saw it. If a person took a hare in this way and pleaded that he had only happened on it by chance, and if that person had no record of poaching, then the bench might very well take a lenient view of the matter.

If the keeper finds a hare in a snare, removes it and concealing all signs simply pulls down the snare, the poacher coming by will imagine that the snare has been knocked down and will re-set it. In such a case there could be no defence for the man, who is caught red-handed.

When a keeper finds a number of broken scraps of white pottery dropped in a seemingly haphazard manner along the foot of a hedge he will notice that each one lies close to a good hare run or smeuse. This is a sure sign that the poacher will return after dark and, using the white flashes as markers, set a snare in each place. Alternatively, a poacher might wander along a hedge during his lunch break cutting slices of turnip for his 'dockey' with his 'shut-knife'. An observant keeper would notice that every so often he allows a slice of turnip to fall to the ground, always near a smeuse. The gleaming white flash at night would be as efficient as a row of beacons, but far less suspicious.

Poachers did not often use pegs to fix their snares, preferring to tie the string directly to a bough in the hedge bottom. This meant the tackle they had to take with them and conceal on their persons was less bulky, while a springy stick on site would deal with a hare more quickly than a peg which might pull out or break.

Snowy weather was a time when the keeper was especially alert, for then it was that game animals became sharp set and hungry and would lose much of their natural fear of man in their search for food. Footprints would provide the lone poacher with the

clearest evidence as to which smeuses were most heavily used, and this information could be used to advantage later. However, it was the case of sauce for the goose, and the poacher's footprints were equally visible to the keeper – so he would see to it that he kept on the right side of the fence.

Both hares and rabbits are especially fond of gnawing green twigs in hard weather, as any tree planter or forester knows, often to his cost. A good poaching trick was to take a green ash stick and plant it upright in the snow in a field known to be popular with hares – no hare could resist this succulent temptation and would come straight over and nibble it. It was a simple matter then for the poacher to hide a set of gin traps in the snow nearby, an especially deadly method.

In snowy conditions, hares could easily be shot at night. They would flock to any remaining stands of root crops or greens, and stood out boldly in the moonlight, looking as large as sheep on the snowy wastes – a hidden gun could account for six or seven of them in a night. In this season the poacher was as likely to be as hungry as the hares, and a good hare would keep a cottager's family in food for some time.

In summer hares were vulnerable, too: at daybreak when heavy dew had fallen, hares would often come out onto the chalky roads to dry their fur and to have a morning warm in the early rays. A crafty man would hide in the hedge bottom with a rusty gun and shoot them as they lolloped past. If he doubted his marksmanship enough not to risk a running shot, he would give a short whistle, at which the hare would invariably stop and look round to see where the noise came from. The best place was a crossroads where hares would congregate; there was the added advantage that the poacher had a choice of routes by which to make his escape should the keeper approach to see who had fired the shot.

THE OAT STUBBLE

Oats are grown less frequently these days, but at one time they were a common crop, used as feed for horses. Hares are especially fond of oat stubbles, and the keeper would watch these closely. A retired farmer lay on the point of death; all his life had been spent in coursing, and wives and estates had run through his hands because of his devotion to his favourite sport. It was widely believed, however, that he had a large amount of money safely concealed – the family was therefore gathered anxiously round his bedside, for there had been no will nor mention of any bequests.

Then with quavering voice the old man called for a favourite nephew; the lad came forward eagerly for what he felt sure was a generous bequest. The old fellow motioned the lad to stoop down so that he might catch every precious word; 'Jimmy, me boy,' said he, 'When you goes a'coursing, always look an oat stubble for a hare' – and so saying, he expired. That was it; the most important gleaning of eighty years, and he was anxious that it was not lost to posterity.

PROTECTING THE HARE FIELD

Advice from John Wilkins.

Set an alarm gun in the field where the hares feed, generally a clover field; place it in the centre of the field and attach three strings to the trigger, leading them away from it in the form of a three cornered table so that the dog is bound to run onto one of the three when driving hares and hunting the field. Bang! goes the gun and off run the poachers. 'He's shot the dog,' they cry and forthwith catch up their nets as quickly as possible and make off. If there are two nets they take the nearest and leave the other and they do not stop to take the gate-netting.

After they have gone about half a mile the dog overtakes them. 'The old Devil missed 'un after all,' is their polite comment. 'That couldn't've been Wilkins shot him, it was one of his men; he'd be a dead 'un if Wilkins rose his gun to him.'

A SHORT BURST

Gil Gaylor has a successful night.

I had set some snares for hares in the hedge gaps. Later that night whilst approaching them, I bolted a hare into one of them and it gave a piercing scream. Quickly I broke its neck and loosened the snare and gathered up the others which were empty.

At this instant a keeper's dog, an old labrador, came bounding up, barking furiously. Grabbing the hare and snares, I leaped through a gap in the hedge and headed across the stubble. A gun went off to scare whoever the keeper thought I was. I reached the roadside safely, then crossed more fields, the dog still barking a field or more away.

HOW TO HOLD HARES

I wouldn't tell the secret once but I will now. Take a pound or more of parsley seed and sow in the night time all over the field. Let no one know anything about it, but take the seed in your large pockets and scatter it broadcast all over the field. The hares will then feed in that field in preference to any other. I have done the same thing on land sown with clover, near the cover; that is, home fields not those a long way from your woods. This is one dodge to make the hares feed at home and take to that particular field for feeding. The hares will keep the parsley down and even if the farmer does find a sprig of parsley in the clover, he will think that it slipped in among the clover seed.

THE TRAVELLER

Another trial for hare and keeper alike was the wandering traveller in a dog cart accompanied by a greyhound. The dog would not be trotting along behind like an honest dog, but curled up and hidden beneath the seats. From his elevated position a driver can easily spot a hare in form in a roadside field, and it is a matter of seconds to slip the dog and grab the hare, sometimes even before she is started. Even if the keeper witnesses this dastardly deed, the poachers are back in the cart and trotting off to safety long before he can come up to them.

POOR MAN'S POTTAGE

In an era in which the fastest mode of transport was a horse and cart, and later a bicycle, village folk learned to use their eyes. Nothing like a bike for teaching you about every bump in the road, for reminding you of every gap in the hedge, where covies rest and the hare likes to sit.

As long as there is game to take, someone will try for it for any one of a number of reasons; it has been going on since the time of William Rufus when the nobles sought to protect their deer and the locals did what they could to thwart them. When mankind ceases to observe the world around him and believes that his control of it is absolute, unlike the poacher and keeper who realised along with all primitive peoples that we must live in harmony with it, the future of our race will be in jeopardy.

THE POACHER'S GUN

The last thing a poacher wanted was a gun licence, for such would proclaim his calling to all and sundry; so all poaching guns were held illegally. A man with a gun walking the village street was doing no more than openly proclaiming his profession, for only the landed gentry were expected to shoot game. A gun would be broken into its two main parts, the stock fitted into one long pocket inside the coat and the barrel inside another, both pockets made especially for that purpose. The barrel would be sawn or filed short the better to fit; this operation severely lowered the weapon's capability of shooting at range, but for a poacher more concerned with 'browning' a sitting covey or firing at a pheasant five yards off in a tree, there was no need to worry about such a consideration.

The Victorian poacher's gun was a muzzle-loader or sometimes a converted flint, as the new-fangled breech-loaders were far too expensive for him. Any keeper worth the name could detect a man encumbered with the two parts of a heavy gun sewn into his coat, although it might escape the notice of a layman. An encounter with the keeper when thus encumbered was to be avoided at all costs. However, the shortened barrel would double as a handy bludgeon if a close battle with keepers was to occur, the gun in such a state probably being just as dangerous as when fully made up and loaded.

On one occasion a poacher's gun fell into the hands of a shooting writer, and it amused him to note how the owner had used his ingenuity to keep his monstrous piece in service. From long use and abuse the lock was quite worn out, and when the hammer was raised to full cock the trigger failed to hold it in position so that it fell back on the nipple. The owner dared not send it for repair, for such an act would expose him as a gun owner and word would spread to the wrong ears.

He therefore drove a nail into the stock near the hammer, cocked the gun, and tied the hammer to the nail with a short length of string. When taking aim the poacher would hold a sharp knife in his right hand and when he wanted to fire he cut the string, which allowed the hammer to fall and thus fired the gun. The business of loading and preparing to fire must have been lengthy and complicated, not to say dangerous. The chronicler remarked drily that the crack shot of the day, Lord de Grey, would have been a trifle slow with his fifth and sixth barrels if he had been obliged to rely on a trio of guns which worked on this principle.

The muzzle-loader could not easily be unloaded like a breech-loading gun, and the poacher would not wish to waste a charge of shot; so he would often dismantle his gun with the charge still in place and the nipple on the cap. Swinging freely in the tail of his secret coat pocket it was not unknown for a man crossing a stile to bang the nipple against a solid object with the result that, with the barrel pointing upwards, he received the whole charge of shot in his body.

THE GROUND GAME ACT, 1880

This gave tenants certain rights regarding hares and rabbits, and if the tenant did not care to shoot them for sport he passed on the right to some local ne'er-do-well. This man became a thorn in the keeper's flesh, with authority to wander over prime game country where he could easily assess the concentrations of feathered game and make his plans for a less official night visit. The sight of the local rat-catcher with half-a-dozen ragged terriers yapping at his heels walking freely next to the master's prime coverts was enough to drive most keepers to apoplexy.

A LIKELY LADY

A keeper's wife with more than her share of feminine intuition became suspicious of an informant who was always coming with sneaking pieces of information about fearful poaching deeds carried out by his work-mates. The keeper was a more simple soul and trusted him. One day this fellow came round as usual and found the keeper not at home; he was out on his rounds. Enquiring as to his whereabouts, he was told by the good woman that 'himself' was ill in bed with a bad head. Wishing him a speedy recovery, the informer departed.

Later that night the same man was frog-marched to the cells, caught in the act of setting snares by the light of a dark lantern, mistakenly thinking himself safe while the keeper was tossing and turning in his 'sick bed'.

STRANGE INFORMATION

A keeper was awoken late at night by a tapping on his window. Below he saw a grizzled veteran poacher, well known to him, who hissed that a gang was netting the big wood and that if he came immediately he would bag the lot of them. Suspecting a try-on, the keeper nevertheless followed the man and asked him the reason for his change of colours.

It was quite simple – the old man had been rejected by his former associates as being past active service. They no longer wanted him with them, and this was his way of taking revenge. The keeper caught the gang who gave in without resistance.

Even the village schoolmaster could be a useful source of information. One such miserable specimen took the keeper aside and whispered that little Tommy Robinson was always bringing cooked hare and pheasant to school for his lunch. As his father was a poor labouring man and could not legitimately come by such fare, this man was one to be closely watched. The schoolmaster was rewarded with a couple of rabbits.

One old woman invited a keeper into her parlour and told him that her cat was always bringing back game bones from her neighbour's ash tip, while the day before she had distinctly smelled burning feathers. The old woman acted so spitefully because she had fallen out with the neighbour's wife, who was 'allus tormenting me'.

Even the chimney sweep might have his uses to the keeper: one sweep once told the head man that when cleaning a certain old gaffer's chimney he had come across a large bundle of rabbit wires hidden in the brick bread oven.

THE GANG

Even harder to bring to book than the solitary poaching labourer was a group of them in league with one another. Almost impregnable, they had many pairs of eyes looking out all the time, were quick to give warnings, and between them refined day poaching to an art.

The trick here was for the keeper to 'befriend' one of them, to take him aside for a confidential chat in full view of his fellows, to slip him the occasional ounce of baccy or a rabbit. This man would never again be fully trusted by his chums, for they feared that he had been made a spy and was the keeper's man, despite all his protestations of innocence.

This trick worked especially well for one particular keeper, new to the job, who was faced with a well-established gang on his estate. He tried to befriend one of the men but with only moderate success. In the end he invited the chap round to his cottage (past the snarling dog) and gave him an hospitable evening. At the end, noticing that his guest's coat had seen better days, he offered him an old suit of his own velveteens which, though far from new, were a good deal better than the rags the man was wearing.

That did the trick, for the man's erstwhile friends were now certain that he was in the keeper's pocket, and their activities ceased. A poacher never felt comfortable in the presence of velveteen; as soon ask a man to commit a burglary with a policeman standing by – even a waxwork one.

THE POACHER'S CLUB

In some areas the poachers formed themselves into an unofficial club so that they could orchestrate their activities and pool all information. This was risky, considering they were such an untrusting and untrustworthy lot, but there *were* times when it was to their advantage. If a captain possessed of authority and a strong personality was appointed, he could divide his area into patches and set various gangs to work them depending on their equipment and expertise.

Half a county could be organised in this way and the keepers led a merry dance, always seeming to be in the wrong place and not knowing why. The game was sold centrally and a third of the profits were set aside as a fund against emergencies of all kinds; for example fines inflicted by the courts were paid from it, lawyers hired in doubtful cases, and maintenance paid to families should their man be sent to prison.

Should a poacher come to court, the captain would see to it that all the other poachers turned up to jeer at the keeper and do their best to sway the opinions of the magistrates in favour of their chum. Not infrequently this was successful, with the 'victim' being represented as a poor man doing his best to feed a large and starving family; a good poacher is also a good actor. The magistrates were too often unaware – then, as now, too – of the many nights the keeper lay in wait, the many times he got wet through, the frustrations, and his courage in facing up to what might well have been an armed and dangerous gang. When the case was over, irrespective of the result, the poachers spent the rest of the day drinking in the local pubs.

Even in the summer the gang would maintain its identity. Members spent the time mending and making nets and other devices, training dogs and seeking casual harvest work on farms. Needless to say this 'honest' work was only a front, which they used to familiarise themselves with the ground for expeditions on winter nights. They tended to live in the nearby towns rather than in the villages where folk have nothing better to do than keep a close watch on the activities of their neighbours. In a town, so long as such a man paid his rates and did not beat his wife too often, he could pass the season beyond suspicion, and be looked on as an eminently respectable citizen.

SIGNS OF TROUBLE

It was not always obvious to a keeper that he was being poached, for the silent poacher on his own who only ever took a few head of game at a time might well have made his depredations for years without detection.

As we have seen, the alarm gun had its advantages, but a skilled poacher could avoid it by keeping away from paths and feeling before him with a reed. The answer was the old dodge of stretching a length of cotton between trees in likely places. The cotton should not be tied too tight or it would snap when wet and stretched, and also the swaying of the trees in a breeze would break it. The thread should be strung too high for a fox to catch it.

Broken threads would not only tell the keeper that there had been a trespasser but, just as important, what direction he had taken – and just as soon as a pattern of movement had been established, an ambush could be set.

WELL-READ POACHERS

In 1938, ten Cardiff men were summoned at Weston-super-Mare for poaching on Steepholm, a small island in the Bristol Channel. It was stated that they journeyed to the island in two small boats with a dog and guns, but on seeing the approach of a motorboat containing police constables and other members of the pursuit party, they took to their boats, hoisting sails as well as oars. In the chase they threw overboard a volume of *Encyclopaedia Brittanica*.

HIGHLAND POACHERS' BEDTIME

From Wild Sports of the Highlands *by Charles St John.*

Hardy and active as the mountain deer, in the company of two or three comrades of the same stamp as himself, he sleeps in the heather wrapped in his plaid regardless of frost or snow and commences his work at daybreak.

When a party of them sleep out on the hill side their manner of arranging their couch is as follows: If snow is on the ground they first scrape it off a small space; they then all collect a quantity of the driest heather they can find. The next step is for all the party excepting one to lie down close to each other with room between one couple for the remaining man to get into the rank when his duty is done – which is, to lay all the plaids on the top of his companions and on the plaids a quantity of long heather. When he has sufficiently thatched them in he creeps into the vacant place and they are made up for the night.

The coldest frost has no effect on them bivouacking in this manner. Their guns are laid dry between them and their dogs share their masters' couch.

With the earliest grouse crow they rise and commence operations. Their breakfast consists of meal and water. They generally take a small bag of meal with them but it is seldom that there is not some good-natured shepherd living near their day's beat who, notwithstanding that he receives pay for keeping off or informing against all poachers, is ready to give them milk and anything else his bothy affords.

OBY ON THE DANGERS OF FIGHT

From The Amateur Poacher *by Richard Jefferies.*

'They used to try and get me to fight the keeper when they did catch me with a wire, but I knowed as hitting is transporting, and just put my hands in my pockets and let 'em do as they liked. *They* knows I beant afraid of 'em in the road; I've thrashed more than one of 'em, but I ain't going to jump into *that* trap.

'I've been before the bench, at one place and 'tother, heaps of times and paid the fine for trespass. Last time the Chairman said to I 'So you be here again, Oby; we hear a good deal about you.' I says, 'Yes, my lard, but people never don't hear nothing about you. That shut the old duffer up. Nobody never heard nothing of he except at rent audit.'

ALMOST A RIGHT AND LEFT

An amateur poacher stood on a public lane and the local constable happened along and engaged him in conversation. The lane was lonely and little used by the public. While they were talking a hare suddenly burst into view and crossed the lane. Up went the gun and over went the hare and the policeman summoned the shooter for discharging a firearm within fifty feet of the highway. When the case came before the court and had been outlined, the defendant turned to the bench and asked:

'If you had been in my place, what would you have done?'

'Well,' murmured the sympathetic Chairman, 'If I had been in your place, I think I would have let the policeman have the second barrel.'

SHOOTING TIMES, 1897

Nothing shows more completely the decadence of poachers, morals than the fact that a man who admits he is an old hand at the game has fallen so low as to steal dead pheasants. An old-fashioned poacher with a pride in his profession would have scorned such an undignified method of acquiring spoil. Thomas Jackson was caught in the act of stealing two dead pheasants from the shop of Mr Webb of Streatham, and when brought before the South Western magistrate said, 'I am an old poacher and have more at home'.

There is, however, a great difference between stealing 'still' game and capturing the flying birds on their native heath. The latter may be wrong, but it has in it an element of sport as well as of danger: but the former, as the magistrate remarked, is simply larcenous impudence. For the offence Jackson was relegated to the treadmill for 14 days.

FARMER WILLUM'S REVENGE

From The Amateur Poacher *by Richard Jefferies.*

As well as the pheasant we shot about half a dozen rabbits, two more hares and a woodpigeon afterwards; but all these were as nothing compared with the woodcock.

How Farmer Willum chuckled over it – especially to think that we had cut out the game from the very batteries of the enemy! It was the one speck of bitterness in the old man's character – his hatred of this keeper. Disabled himself by age and rheumatism from walking far, he heard daily reports from his men of this fellow coming over the boundary to shoot, or drive pheasant and partridge away. It was a sight to see Farmer Willum stretch his bulky length in his old armchair right before the middle of the great fire of logs on the hearth, twiddling his thumbs and every now and then indulging in a hearty laugh, followed by a sip at the 'straight cup'.

Peter Hawker's Poaching

Colonel Peter Hawker was the father of English wildfowling. Ex-officer of Wellington's army, he devoted his life to punt gunning and pursuing Hampshire partridges and other game. He was a good shot and a tireless gunner, despite poor health. He wrote two classic shooting books, Instructions to Young Sportsmen *and his* Diaries: 1802 – 1853 *from which the following extracts are taken.*

Parson Bond never allowed anyone a day's shooting and had man traps and dog gins all over his wood. I had made out a regular plan of attack and line of march, but our precision was frustrated by the first man we saw on reaching the ground, who was the keeper. We therefore had not time to hold a council of war, but rushed into cover like a pack of foxhounds before his face. Away he went, naming everyone he could and we all joined him in the hue and cry of 'Where is Parson Bond?'

In the meantime the *feu de joie* was going on most rapidly. At last up came the parson almost choked with rage. The two first people he warned off were Pearson and myself; having been served with notices we kept him in tow while the others rallied his covers and serenaded him with an incessant bombardment in every direction. The confused rector did not know which way

to run. The scene of confusion was ridiculous beyond anything and the invasion of an army would scarcely exceed the noise.

Not a word could be heard for the cries of 'Mark!' 'Dead!' and 'Well Done!' interspersed at every moment with a bang and the yelping of barrack curs. The parson at last mustered his whole establishment to act as patriots against the marauders, footboys running one way, ploughmen mounted on cart horses galloping the other, and everyone from the village that could be mustered was collected to repel the mighty shock.

At last we retreated and about half past four, those that had escaped being entered in his doomsday book renewed the attack. The parson having eased himself by a vomit began to speak more coherently and addressed himself to those who, being liable in the action of trespass were obliged to stand on the footpath and take the birds as they flew over; at last so many were caught that the battle ceased. Though a large number of pheasants were destroyed, the chase did not end in such aggregate slaughter as we expected and not much more than a third of those brought down were bagged, in consequence of our being afraid to turn off our best dogs.

We brought away some of the Parson's traps one of which was a most terrific engine and now hangs in the mess room for public exhibition. Only one dog was caught the whole day, and whose should it be but Parson Bond's!

LITTLE DODGES

John Wilkins had many tricks up his sleeve…

When gate net watching I used to leave rather early and before going away I always knocked the ashes out of my pipe on to the top of the gate leaving the tobacco there smouldering. If any poachers came they would smell the tobacco and suspect that I was still in the neighbourhood watching.

Often too in the woods I have left two or three sticks with old coats hung on them stuck up at the cross rides. Sometimes I have left my lanthorn burning all night with the bulls eye turned on in the watch hut with three or four great coats or horse rugs lying about. All these dodges are very necessary as the poacher coming after your game is very suspicious and does not want to be caught, so that if he sees a light you may be sure that he will give it a wide berth rather than go and see if you are there.

BRADFORD WOOD

More trouble for Colonel Hawker.

A note from Squire Jones to request I would desist from sporting in these fields or near Bradford Wood as they were preserved and telling me he was authorised to 'forbid all trespassers', notwithstanding the whole town shot constantly over them and he had previously given his approbation to my shooting and I had even robbed myself to supply him with game.

MY ANSWER

DEAR SIR — As to my certain knowledge every fellow in this town shoots in the neighbourhood of Bradford Wood, I am almost induced to think you are joking when you call it a preserve. I regret, however, that you were not a day sooner in your application, as I have this moment returned with the only remaining birds (fourteen) in my bag; four brace of which I was on the point of sending to you when I received your note and consequently disposed of them otherwise. I am, etc.

P.S. — I have also countermanded the sending for a capital pointer bitch of which I had promised myself the pleasure of making you a present!

The squire sent a verbal message that I was 'no gentleman'.

(*An increasingly acrimonious correspondence flashed back and forth between Hawker and Squire Jones, the affair ending only when Hawker was obliged to move from the area on military business. Hawker's final missive contained the remark '… being obliged to take my farewell of Bradford early tomorrow, I am prevented from beating the remainder of the manor which otherwise, upon my honour, I most assuredly would have done …'*)

Do-It-Yourself Muzzle-Loader

Alfred Curtis here tells of his father, a keeper-turned-poacher. At one stage of his life, times were so hard that he had been obliged to pawn his gun, his most cherished possession.

Somebody gave him an old muzzle-loader that had lost its hammer. Father didn't bother to get one, he simply loaded up and took with him a crony with hand well bandaged in a piece of rag and holding a lump of iron. Father would come into the field where the rabbits were, stalk them, put a cap on the gun and take aim. While the gun was at his shoulder his pal would lean over. 'Hit it!' Father would hiss, and George would smack down on the cap, and many a rabbit they brought home shot in that way, without a hammer on the gun.

From Little Acorns

Alfred recalls catching birds by varying methods.

At other times and when conditions were right, I took ducks with acorns. It was a cruel method but then so are many of the ways civilised people use to slaughter their food. There was a family at home waiting for me to return with the next meal and I knew how to obtain it.

I hardened my heart, gathered a handful of acorns, made a split along their length, inserted a fish hook into the slit with the barb projecting and a short length of line attached to the other end. Then down I went to the shallows under the oaks where acorns had fallen into the water's edge and there I set my acorn traps and left them while I hid a hundred yards upstream for ducks will not feed unless they see the bank is free. Before long a duck would swim in, and then a

fluttering and splashing of water told me I had made a catch and I hurried over to put it out of its misery. Some time later the keeper in the park remarked that the ducks seemed fewer than usual at this time of year. I forbore comment.

CAUGHT BIRD CATCHING

No sooner was the keeper's back turned than I picked up the brace bird, slipped off the brace and threw it away and let it go free. I did the same with the second, but as I threw the bird into the air Hughie turned and saw me and back he came at a run. 'Look at that!' Hughie cried in disgust; 'He's done away with the evidence.' He towered over me so threateningly that I thought he was going to knock me down, but I knew I could go easy as he had no evidence against me. Then I remembered something, the chaffinch I had caught and the other brace bird in the store cage.

Picking up the store cage I set off towards the hedge then, with some yards start I swerved and tore off across the field ripping off the lid of the cage as I ran, trying to shake the birds out. One I saw take to the air and freedom then the men were upon me.

'He's cheated us again' Hughie cried. 'What's this though, a chaffinch with a broken leg. Come on, we're taking you in.'

A CLEVER STAG POACHER

A team of keepers was watching a fine royal stag when suddenly it collapsed and fell to the bullet of a hidden poacher. The rascal remained out of sight and the keepers held their ground and waited, quite certain that the poacher would not leave such fine booty unretrieved. They decided the their presence had gone undetected and that if they laid an ambush the poacher would be certain to show himself as soon as he felt the coast was clear. Secretly they disposed themselves, two near the carcase and two more by the road which ran nearby.

It was a cold but moonlit night and the four men were chilled with cold; but eventually, after a long wait, the poacher appeared on open ground – he made no attempt at concealment, but walked towards the stag and started hurling rocks at it. The two keepers hiding by the carcase withstood the bombardment manfully until one of them received a direct hit and could not resist groaning. At this the poacher beat a smart retreat over the brow of the hill, the four keepers in hot pursuit; but they lost him in the thick stuff beyond.

Slowly and mournfully they returned to the stag to drag it back to the larder, and were surprised – although they should not have been – to find it gone. The oh-so-obvious poacher had been but a decoy to lure them away while confederates with a pony had slipped in and removed the beast. It turned out afterwards that the poacher had, all along, been aware of the keepers' presence and the whole thing had been a set-up to remove them from the scene.

RISKS OF A HIDDEN GUN

In 1895, New Year's Day, one George Pollock of Milton was walking along Kirkintilloch Road when he met Alexander Scobie, a notorious poacher, in the company of others of similar bent. There was an animated conversation during which it appears that Scobie had been asking the others to 'stand treat' when his gun slipped from inside his coat, the charge went off, and completely destroyed Pollock's right foot.

THE POACHER AFLOAT

The bargee had many opportunities, gliding on his boat silently between green banks and through grassy meadows. His lurcher dog would trot on the tow-path and he had a gun somewhere on board close to hand. He would have the chance of the odd duck, something denied to most poachers: he came to know where they sat, and would be ready to knock down a couple as his craft slid silently round the bend.

CHIPPY SMITH'S PHEASANT

A tale sent me by Mr 'Chippy' Smith of Plymouth. He describes himself charmingly as 'part-time keeper; now seventy-six – but still remembers!'

We were just fifteen and were always watching an old cock pheasant that went to roost on the pear tree in the corner of a market garden. How to bag it was always on our minds.

Then one day we found an old muzzle-loader in my mate's shed; here was our answer. Obtaining powder and a fuse was no problem as both our parents worked in the coal mines and they used to keep all the shot-firing gear at home in them days.

One day we cut some lead into many bits and began to prime the gun. It had no firing mechanism, so after pouring in the gunpowder, we laid a slow-burning fuse, then set a wad of old paper over our homemade shot, topped with another wad.

Creeping down to the pear tree, there he was; all we had to do was light the fuse, aim and down he would come. The question was, who was going to hold the gun. As it was my mate's I told him he could fire it, but he got scared, so we decided to tie it up to the top rail of the fence, aim and stand back.

We made a good job of securing it with plenty of binder twine, and after carefully checking the aim we lit the fuse and dropped down into the ditch. After about two minutes there was one helluva bang and smoke: we heard the old cock take off, and when we looked, part of the fence was missing and as for the gun – we never found a bit of it.

BARE AS A CHICKEN

Mr Oakley from Southend-on-Sea recalls a raid on a hen house.

Ed had decided to pinch a couple of chickens from a local chicken house. Earlier he had purchased a tin of sulpher from the chemist, which when mixed with a secret substance of his own produced an anaesthetic gas. The idea of this was to knock the chickens out so that he could take his pick in peace and quiet without any of the hysterical shrieking that they would inevitably make and which would lead to an ounce of no 7 shot in his rear.

Ed hurdled a few garden fences and scurried through some back yards without a noise, reached the hen house and lit his sulpher. He lifted the small hatch door and slipped the smouldering tin inside. After ten minutes all was silent and the chickens were fast asleep. In order to squeeze through the impossibly small doorway, Ed had to remove all his clothes – with a good deal of bad language and biting his bottom lip he just managed to struggle in. However, just as the last part of his anatomy passed into the chicken house, the hatch dropped shut with a bang. Since there wasn't a handle on the inside, he was stuck.

After a couple of hours the chickens began to wake up, and as they did so, they were not pleased to see a large, bare intruder in their house. The flapping and squawking that followed awoke the owner who came down to find Ed frozen with cold and covered in feathers. Needless to say he sent Ed on his way by whacking his rear end with a broom handle. Ed didn't seem to have found time to put on his clothes.

ED THE OPPORTUNIST

There are many other little tricks that Ed knows, such as going to his local shoot and sneaking in at the back of the guns about a hundred yards behind them and shooting the birds that they miss. Then his girlfriend would run out, pick up the birds and tie them under her big coat. [Sounds familiar! J.H.] When the whistle went for the end of the drive they would make their exit. Sometimes he would get more birds than the guns.

THE CATAPULT MAN

Jim Knight meets a 'man of the woods' in his days at Thetford Chase.

Meeting the man next day he took from his pockets three rabbits in order to be able to sit in comfort. They had clearly not been shot or wired. He went to his inside pocket: 'Here's me little gun.' I had expected anything bar a catapult. The 'prodger' was of holly, near black and smooth as ivory: he said he had had it since he was a lad. Squirrels were plentiful on the Chase and it wasn't long before one fell to his lead shot. Luck? No, it wasn't. He took out several more over the weeks. I saw him squeak up a doe rabbit to within eighteen yards and it was dead.

He was without doubt an expert with this weapon; I had thought catapults were only for bruising your thumb with. He told me he shot about two brace of birds a fortnight for the officers mess at USAF Lakenheath in exchange for tinned food and tobacco. He said, and I could believe him 'I can lift their hats off their heads at twenty yards'.

He added, 'All you bloody 'kippers' are the same; out night and morning looking for poachers. The real ones come during the day, 10am to 3pm, and I have poached with a keeper in the same field, taken rabbits from his back gate when he's been gardening, and even removed a brace and a hare from the game cart on a shooting day. In the evenings I stir 'em up a bit by cycling round the lanes and leading them astray.

In the end the removal lorry came and he had a last look round 'his' forest. 'Goodbye, old friend' I said, 'give me your new address and I'll write to you.' 'Bain't no bloody good, I cannot read or write – but if I come this way again I'll look you up.' As I write I can hear Danny saying those words. What a lovely old man of the woods, and what a keeper he would have made.

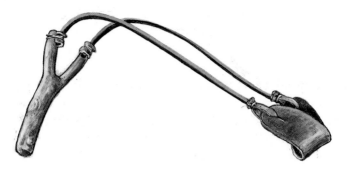

Coot Rig, American Style

The end of World War II saw the introduction of a no feeding or 'baiting' rule within two hundred yards of a 'blind' (hide). Coincidentally there were huge numbers of balsa-wood life-rafts for which no-one had any further use. The hunters designed a pipe frame with a hundred or so blocks of balsa, painted black, attached to it. These coot rigs were anchored over feed at the regulation 200 yards from the blind; when the gunners came to shoot, the rig was moved close to the blind, telling the birds that the food had moved and, consequently, bringing them within range of the guns.

The Norfolk Game Dealer in 1900

Durrant the game dealer was well liked by all who knew or dealt with him. He dealt fairly with the gunners but was too easy-going with the customers, many of them ran accounts with him and some were very slow to pay. In the end, in his old age, he became an honourable bankrupt and much sympathy was shown to him.

Wildfowl and game appealed to him more than rare birds; over the latter he sometimes lost and more rarely made a satisfactory profit. He dealt largely with pheasants and other game and occasionally had setbacks in this direction as cold storage had not yet come into being. His stalls, facing each other in Yarmouth Market were, in the shooting season, besieged by collectors, bird-stuffers, walking gunners, punters and on Saturdays by country sportsmen who were usually poachers in a small way, for they brought in hares or longtails of their own or another's getting. Transactions were usually carried out behind the stalls with all the secrecy of bookmakers' touts at street corners. Many a small canvas bag went away empty in coat-tail pockets.

Saturdays were a great delight to me and others who kept a keen eye on the geese, swans, ducks and waders that hung in rows or in bunches on one stall, hares and pheasants on the other. He sometimes offered fixed prices for snipe when orders were many, at other times for woodpigeons, plovers and so on. When snipe were exceptionally abundant, prices were low, after protracted frosts, lower still. On one particular occasion so many snipes were brought him that after giving three-ha'pence each for them, he lost on his deals. When these birds were scarce and orders came in for them, it is more than probable that 'stints' (dunlins) whose standard price was a penny each to the gunners, found their way upon the table of the snipe-lovers.

TEAMWORK

Women folk were often used to act as porters for poaching gear. The smartly dressed lady with the capacious Gladstone bag could well be taking a set of snares and pegs to another member of the gang, and she would pass the closest scrutiny. Meanwhile the gang members would have left for their various destinations, unencumbered by incriminating material which would be left for them in a rick or under a culvert at the scene of their operation. A keeper who happened on such a cache was well advised to hide nearby, and would probably be able to make an arrest. He could also make allies of those trusted workers who lived in outlying cottages on the estate. Such informants could be most useful; but the keeper should not be seen talking to any of them, for fear of arousing suspicion. The problem of breaking up the well-organised network of such a gang, with its diffuse systems of moving game, hiding equipment and avoiding arrest, was a great one.

The poaching gang had anticipated by many years the Mafia, in its system of dividing a large area into patches; and also the unions, by operating a one-for-all and all-for-one system of mutual protection.

ONE OF MR TULLY'S USEFUL RECIPES

Oils to Draw Rabbits and Hares:
Oil of Parsley, quarter ounce.
Oil of Angelica, 1 dram.
Oil of Aniseed, half dram.
Oil of Copaiba, half ounce.
Mix; Put a few drops on pieces
of wood and lay about.

Diving Duck Trap,
Chesapeake Bay, Maryland

My friend and correspondent Phil Williamson of Cambridge, Maryland, sends me information about American wildfowl poachers and their ingenuity.

The duck trap was built on the lines of our familiar crow and magpie letter-box trap. A rectangular cage of mesh on a wooden framework some ten feet by five, and deep enough to stick well above the surface of the water, was lowered into a shallow bay where diving duck congregated. These birds fed by diving to the bottom and pulling weed or clams; they were good underwater swimmers and could stay submerged for long periods.

Well in advance the area was baited with corn and suchlike special treats; in time the duck followed the food trail, entered the trap at some submerged point and found themselves unable to escape. The poacher had only to leave his trap which would work for him on its own, and return the next day by boat and collect his bag.

ARTHUR'S POACHER

Arthur Cadman is a great fowler, game shot, international deer expert, naturalist and all-round countryman. In his time he has come across a plethora of tales of old poachers. This is a sample of a personal encounter.

Last Wednesday I was sitting in a high seat as a guest waiting for a buck to come out from a large area of hardwood to feed in a lush field of wheat. The nearest point of the wood was about 65 yards from me, the furthest end of the wood within my view was about 200 yards away. By 7pm I was expecting a deer to emerge at any moment. Already a hare had come out 110 yards away.

Suddenly I saw a man creeping down the edge of the wood from the furthest point on my right. The glasses revealed that he had a high-powered rifle with scope slung across his back. In his hands he held a twelve-bore at the ready. He was walking downwind, giving his wind to the whole wood! 'Not a very efficient poacher,' was my mental note. I was in full view of him had he used his eyes, but he had no field glasses.

When he was 50 yards from the hare, it ran away, towards me. The man crouched down. 'If he shoots the hare with his rifle I could end up in the game larder,' I thought. Luckily he did not take the rifle from his back but continued his stalk. My seat was a very awkward one to get off and my running days are over. I debated what I should do. Perhaps the man was a friend of my host. When the man was at the nearest point, I quacked like a mallard. The man spun round and saw me at once; he was nonplussed.

He retreated fast for thirty yards and then decided that I could never catch him. He laid down both rifle and gun, took out a large handkerchief and mopped his brow. Then he lit a cigarette, obviously pondering the situation. A moment later he picked up his weapons and retreated as fast as he could, back from whence he had come.

Needless to say no buck came out: the hare took an hour and a quarter to return. I was able to give my host an accurate and detailed description of the poacher who was unknown to him. But he was fairly certain that he would soon find out who he was!

Peacock Pie

How to remove a peacock from the lawn of a stately home without anyone noticing. Hugh, the gardener's boy, no more than a lad, had set his heart on possessing this beautiful bird.

One afternoon the boy put the dregs of a whiskey bottle on a picking of chicken meal and laid it on the flags of the path, keeping watch from the herb plot where he made a pretence at working with a hoe. The peacock came. Its beak darted at the drops of meal. In a little while the bird was stupefied and Hugh quickly ran and tied a sugar bag over its head. For the rest of the afternoon the peacock sat in drunken contemplation under a laurel bush.

Could he have some geranium cuttings? begged little Hugh. The under-gardener considered and then gave consent. The peacock left its ancestral home in a sack from which geranium cuttings protruded through a conspicuous hole.

187

THE LAST WORD

A retired keeper pays tribute to his old adversary

The true poacher is a person who fully understands wildlife and woodcraft, also the habits of his fellow man, the keeper. He uses the habits of one to help him catch the other. He needs no weapons or help of any kind. He is without doubt a master of his art. Envied by keepers who fail to understand him, they lust to have his knowledge to add to their own.

The sun is his clock, the sky his roof and the birds and beasts his constant companions: they grew up together. He is a mine of information on all creatures and plants. He has respect for all. He will come and go like a ghost of the night, taking only his needs. I raise my hat to this man; he is part of our countryside.

May he still be with my great grandchildren together on our land.

JAMES KNIGHT
(Retired keeper; Yeovil, Somerset)

EPILOGUE

So there they are, a mixed bag of rascals, genuine old countrymen, desperate labourers, artists, ragamuffins, and mouchers. Are they as bad as Payne Gallwey made out? Are they as saintly as Richard Jefferies would have us believe? There is no answer, for as in most callings of men there are some good and some bad. As I made clear in my introduction, the rural terrorists who know nothing of the woods and fields but who come mob-handed to raid woods and offer violence do not deserve the name poacher. However, there are others who earned even the grudging respect of the keepers, their sworn enemies. There are many accounts herein of poachers becoming good keepers, being befriended and often reformed; there was a mutual recognition of like souls.

Let us allow them to melt away into the mist by the side of a straggling hedge, for it is twilight for them. As they go their silent ways, peering here and there to note the 'smeuses' or staring into the quickthorn for the ragged shape of a roosting pheasant, leave them in peace for, as they fade from our sight they fade also into history for there are very few of them left.

As for me, I prefer to pull up the blankets, roll over in bed and go to sleep when the owls hoot, the wind howls in the eaves and the moon floats up like a white balloon above the tossing sea of the oaks.

189

BIBLIOGRAPHY

I acknowledge the following works from which material has been quoted. My task would have been impossible without them.

The Diary of Colonel Peter Hawker (Kingsmead, 1893)
Doyle, Lynn. *Ballygullion* (Penguin, 1942)
Hopkins, Harry *The Long Affray* (Secker & Warburg, 1985)
Jefferies, Richard. *The Amateur Poacher* (Tideline,1879)
Martin, Brian P. *Tales of the Old Gamekeepers* (David & Charles, 1989)
Niall, Ian. *The New Poacher's Handbook* (Heinemann, 1960)
Nudds, Angus. *The Woods Belong to Me* (Blandford Press, 1985)
Patterson, Arthur. *Wildfowlers and Poachers* (Methuen, 1929)
Payne Gallwey, Sir Ralph. *Shooting (Badminton Library)* (Longman, 1886)
Poachers versus Keepers (Gilbertson and Page, 1894)
Rider Haggard, Lilias. *I Walked by Night* (Nicholson & Watson, 1935)
Roberston, James Irvine (ed.). *Random Shots – the first fifty years of Shooting Times*
    (Pelham, 1990)
St. John, Charles. *Wild Sports of the Highlands* (John Murray, 1893)
Scrope, William. *Days and Nights of Salmon Fishing* (Arnold, 1898)
Speakman, Fred and Alfred Curtis. *A Poacher's Tale* (Bell, 1961)
Walsh, Harry M. *The Outlaw Gunner* (Tidewater, USA, 1971)
Wentworth Day, James. *Sporting Adventure* (Harrap, 1937)
Wilkins, John. *An English Gamekeeper* (Sporting & Leisure Press,1892)
Willock, Colin. *Kenzie, the Wild Goose Man* (Andre Deutsch,1962)

Open Field Magazine
The Shooting Times and Country Magazine

ACKNOWLEDGEMENTS

My special thanks to the following who sent me their own fascinating reminiscences.

Arthur Cadman – all-round countryman.
Gil Gaylor – the self-proclaimed Gatcombe Woods Poacher.
James Knight – the retired keeper from Somerset.
Charles Oakley from Southend.
Chippy' Smith from Plymouth.
 Mrs Pat Walker, widow of 'Dick'.
Phil Williamson from Cambridge, Maryland.

   I also acknowledge the many famous books from which I have taken unique poaching yarns of long ago. What would a good book on poaching be if it did not poach tales from other books on the same subject?

JOHN HUMPHREYS
Bottisham

INDEX

INDEX